Supporting Families

Through Meaningful Ministry

purposeful design®
PUBLICATIONS

Colorado Springs, Colorado

D'Arcy Maher, Editor

Purposeful Design Publications is the publishing division of the Association of Christian Schools International (ACSI) and is committed to the ministry of Christian school education, to enable Christian educators and schools worldwide to effectively prepare students for life. As the publisher of textbooks, trade books, and other educational resources within ACSI, Purposeful Design Publications strives to produce biblically sound materials that reflect Christian scholarship and stewardship and that address the identified needs of Christian schools around the world.

Unless otherwise identified, all Scripture quotations are taken from the Holy Bible, New International Version©. Copyright © 1973, 1978, 1984 by Biblica, Inc. All rights reserved worldwide. Used by permission.

Scripture quotations marked (NASB) are taken from the New American Standard Bible. Copyright © 1960, 1962, 1963, 1968, 1971, 1972, 1973, 1975, 1977, 1995 by The Lockman Foundation. Used by permission.

Scripture quotations marked (NKJV) are taken from the Holy Bible, New King James Version (NKJV). Copyright © 1982 by Thomas Nelson, Inc. Used by permission. All rights reserved.

Printed in the United States of America
19 18 17 16 15 14 13 12 11   1 2 3 4 5 6 7

Maher, D'Arcy, editor
    Supporting families through meaningful ministry
    ISBN 978-1-58331-382-4 Catalog #6630

Design team: Bethany Kerstetter, Mike Riester
Editorial team: Sue Grise, John Conaway

Purposeful Design Publications
A Division of ACSI
PO Box 65130 • Colorado Springs CO 80962-5130
Customer Service: 800-367-0798 • www.acsi.org

This compilation of *Christian Early Education* (*CEE*) magazine articles was created to support your intentional practices as you work with and nurture young children.

We in ACSI Early Education Services dedicate this book to you, the enthusiastic Christian early educators who nurture young children to the glory of God.

Contents

vii   Introduction

Section 1: Mission POSSIBLE

3   From Overlooked to Oasis: The Power of Your Mission
Susannah Wayland in collaboration with Carol Damschroder

7   Just Who Is a Child's First Teacher?
Larry Bogle

13   More than Just Words: Do Your Classrooms Reflect Your Philosophy?
Tina Daigre

17   The Power of the Christian School Community
Julia Wurst

Section 2: Practical Tools

23   How Are We Doing? Assessing Parent Ministry Components
Leanne Leak

29   The Family Connection
D'Arcy Maher

33   Informing Parents About Teaching Through Experiences
D'Arcy Maher

37   The Message Was Sinking In
Jim Ed Hardaway

41   The Virtue Tree: Shaping Children as Moral Doers
Teena Ingram

45   Home Visits: Why Do Them?
Becky Lockwood

49   "Mommy Come Get Me?"
Paula Cowart

53   Active Dads = Increased Investment
Darlene Buchanan Bladon

55   Creating a Bond Between Parents and Teachers
Stacia Emerson

59   Keys to Communication
Dorothy Brunson

61   Supporting Military Families
Pamela Flannery

65   Make the Connection: Parental Involvement in Education
Sara Jo Dillard

71   Love with a Purpose: Helping Preschool Families Deal with Grief
Danny Oertli

73   Building a Bridge of Trust: The Parent-Teacher Partnership
Susan Mathis

77   The "New Normal" Family
Elisa Morgan

Section 3: Parent Education Resources

87   Patient Parent vs. Pushy Parent
Milton Uecker

93   How to "Stress Proof" Your Child
Mary Campbell

99   Raising a Musical Child
Catherine Santander

101   Appropriately Engaged or Playing Helicopter?
Ken Smitherman

103   Effectively Communicating with Your Child's Teacher
Carol Kautz

105   The Pitfalls of Over-scheduling our Children
Carol Kautz

107   Meeting Your Child's Need for Love
Carla Foote

111   "Mommy, What Are You Eating?"
Carla Foote

115   Roots of Green Values
Carla Foote

117   Cornering the Market: Out-of-the-Box Possibilities
Carla Foote

121   Program or Process: Spiritual Development in Our Children
Carla Foote

125   Parenting Through Pain
Carla Foote

127   "But Mom, You Promised!" The Responsibility Gene
Carla Foote

Introduction

Why Another Early Education Book?

Intentional practices. *Intentionality* is perhaps one of the loveliest words in the English language. It encompasses *purpose*, *planning*, *meaningfulness*, *nuance*, *creativity*, and *capacity*. Its opposites, such as *chance* and *accident*, clarify the definition even more. When we bring the beauty of this word into the early education classroom, teaching practices elevate the experience of the child. Learning occurs and growth emerges.

Distinctly Christian programs. Those programs that chose to include a faith distinctive enjoy the unfettered opportunity to integrate and celebrate the life of Christ and the words of Scripture throughout the entire program. Does your program embrace this reality? Does your team strive to know Christ and make Him known throughout every part of the day?

Perhaps this book will breathe new life and excitement into your endeavors to create a program that is even more distinctly Christian.

A common language: ministry. There is no dearth of quality early education resources. The field is blessed with competent and capable authors on many topics. We applaud their work.

Our commitment to you, however, is to approach each topic from a distinctly biblical worldview and to share any message in our common language: ministry to children and families. This common focus binds us together in a passionate commitment to this ministry. Will you explore this book, written in the language of ministry, with your team?

Careful stewardship. Over the years, we have been blessed to have exemplary practitioners and academicians write for *Christian Early Education* magazine. Because the magazine is a cornerstone of the ACSI Early Education Department, we sometimes overlook the fact that this piece often fails to reach classroom teachers and teacher assistants.

As stewards of this archive, we've compiled relevant, topical articles that are accessible to any early educator—without the barrier of a subscription. We've enriched the offerings and added a CD of rich resources.

Wander among the pages. Download the resources. Enjoy!

Essential Beliefs of ACSI Early Education

Children are a gift from God. Procreation is an awesome privilege and responsibility, and it is God's provision for the continuation of humankind. Rather than seeing a statistic, we view each child as a gift with talents, potential, and purpose. Each child is carefully crafted by God; parents welcome, protect, and pray for their children and introduce them to the world in which they all live. Parents serve as stewards of the gift of their children

Psalms 139:13–16,127:3–5

Parents are children's primary teachers. God lovingly gives children to parents, who serve as the children's first teachers by coaching the children in self-care (feeding, walking, bathing, etc.), introducing them to their environment, and providing an example of basic living skills. Throughout children's lives, parents retain responsibility for them and serve as their primary influences and teachers, whether positive or negative. Scripture validates this role by providing clear instructions on how parents should intentionally guide children.

Deuteronomy 4:9, 6:4–9; Psalm 78:5–6

Changing family structures provide rich opportunities for ministry. God's intent for a family consists of a godly father and a godly mother equally committed to raising their children. Reality, however, reminds us of the many single-parent homes, of adopted children, and of children raised by extended family, by guardians in foster care, in families that reflect postmodern cultural extremes, and by parents who are detached and disengaged. We remember that God loves each individual intensely, that the gospel message reflects God's heart of redemption, and that we are to be salt and light in a dark world.

Romans 5:8, Luke 4:14–21, Matthew 5:13–16

Quality early education programs support the success of children and families. Children bear the consequences of the decisions of their parents, whether positive or negative. Children cannot be held accountable for their parents' decisions; consequently, Christian early educators should not show favoritism to a child from an advantaged setting or judgment to a child from a disadvantaged setting. Rather, Christian early education programs strive to intersect with the lives of children and families in the same way that Christ would if He were serving in that program. Christian early education programs can support families through a wealth of resources by providing parent training, connecting families to valuable programs in local churches, or referring families to organizations within the program's wide faith-based network. Because they recognize that God places the responsibility for a child on the parents, Christian early educators partner with parents and guardians for the benefit of the child.

Luke 19:10, 2 Corinthians 2:14–15, Galatians 6:2, 9–10

Christ's example and His teaching on children must infuse every interaction. Christ's attention to children provides a glimpse into the heart of God. Though small and vulnerable, children represent the kingdom of God, and we are to become like them. Christ welcomed children, blessed them, advocated for them to disapproving adults, pronounced judgment on those who would cause them to sin, and identified them as those who exemplify greatness in the kingdom.

Mark 9:33–37, 42; Matthew 18:1–6, 10; Matthew 19:13–15

Essential Values of ACSI Early Education

Dynamic, authentic expressions of biblical principles. The design of all activities and experiences (the whole of what happens in the program) begins with the intent of integrating the truths of Scripture into every aspect of the program. Do all routines, transitions, mealtimes, exploration activities, and instruction support the emergence of biblical principles and teachable moments? Biblical principles become living principles when they are expressed in the lives of teachers and not isolated within the curriculum.

The value of all children. Every child is a unique and special creation from the hand of God. Children in a community of learners gain appreciation for children of different cultures, genders, and abilities as a result of the value that the adults in program leadership place on each child.

The value of the early childhood years. Child development is a unique and complex process. Childhood, the journey through which children travel, is honored as a God-ordained process characterized by unique and distinct development; therefore, early education programs intentionally provide optimum learning experiences for the whole child—experiences that include spiritual, social, emotional, physical, and cognitive development. The process is meaningful.

The valued role of parents and family. Recognizing the importance of parents as the primary educators of their children, the early childhood program supports and intentionally encourages parent partnership in the educational and spiritual formation process.

The value of age-appropriate experiences. Just as God gave Jesus time to grow and develop, so we acknowledge that children need time to develop. Development is not hurried; neither is it left to chance. On the basis of Scripture and best practices, early educators intentionally plan experiences that will have great meaning at the age levels in each classroom.

The significance of accessibility. In Scripture, Jesus was accessible to children. The teacher-child relationship is the cornerstone of a successful early education experience. Early educators embrace their role in reflecting God's intense delight in children through quality interactions that are personal and individualized and that reflect deeply interested and sensitive adults.

The goal of serving disadvantaged families. Poverty reduces the choices of parents to meet the needs of their children in every area (e.g., health, lodging, nourishment, education) by limiting opportunities and alternatives. Throughout Scripture, care for those on the margins of society—the poor, the downtrodden, the immigrant, the orphan, the widow—is expected of believers. Early educators find creative ways to engage disadvantaged families and children, and they seek to mitigate the effects of poverty through fully trained staff members who are sensitive in planning and interactions as they address the needs of the community.

Section 1:
Mission POSSIBLE

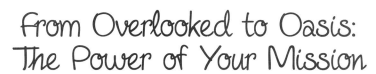

From Overlooked to Oasis: The Power of Your Mission

By Susannah Wayland in collaboration with Carol Damschroder.
Reprinted from *CEE*, September 2009.

Caring for young children must be responsive, reciprocal, and respectful. These "three Rs" make the preschool classroom a resource in times of crisis for children who may have instability in their home life. In today's ever-changing world, family crises and chaos can come in many different forms: financial hardship, job loss, marital problems, single parenting, and health issues. Dual-income parents have work schedules that they need to coordinate. These issues, like spilled milk, cannot be overlooked when caring for children in a Christian childcare setting.

Our mission is to love the Lord, to love the families we serve, and to be willing to help soak up the spilled milk alongside them when needed. It starts with the greeting, it is supported in the environment, and it continues through intentional ministry to both the children and the families.

3

Greeting Cain

Your first connection with the children and their families begins with the greeting. This greeting is an important time to connect with the children. Let the children know—through your voice, facial features, and physical touch—that you are so glad they are here. Getting down at the eye level of the children to greet them also allows you to do a quick health check. Conversing with the parents to obtain important details of care for the day provides comfort for the children and gives the parents confidence and closure before they leave to begin their day.

It is vitally important that we as early educators consider our greeting and that we attempt to personalize it to each family's special needs. As an assistant director, I had the daily drop-off routine of greeting families as I opened car doors and helped unbuckle the children. One mother, alone in Columbus while her husband worked miles away, had autistic twins and a typically developing three-year-old. This drop-off routine gave young Cain a sense of autonomy and gave his mother the security she needed to cope with her situation. She could give me important details I needed

to know after Cain had left the car and still have her autistic boys secure in the car. Within minutes she would then leave to take her twins across town to their special school.

Protecting Adam

Policies and procedures at the center need to be in place so that we always address health concerns and keep communication clear. A parent who brings a child who has medical issues needs the security of knowing that the center has a solid foundation and that the center is intentional and purposeful about meeting special needs every day. Currently in our center an infant we will call Adam has multiple allergies that require a special diet. Each morning the teacher must listen closely to the single mom's instructions and make sure all the details of the infant's diet are written down on a daily sheet. We must clearly label food in the refrigerator so that no mistakes occur. One mistake could cause misery for Adam, a sleepless night for Mom, and perhaps the hardship of her having to take a precious sick day in order to secure medical treatment.

Comforting Emma

We must consider the importance of the environment we create for all our infants, toddlers, and preschoolers, but especially those in chaos or crisis. First and foremost, their environment must be safe and clean and supportive of children's basic needs. The environment, which needs to include child-size items for the children, must be comfortable and able to stimulate exploration and creativity. The schedule of the day should be flexible yet routine and predictable. We should create learning opportunities in every center of the room. When children feel safe and secure in their environment, they can feel free to explore—an activity that leads to learning key concepts in a developmentally appropriate way. Dramatic play allows children to act out the adult world on their terms with their peers. When the classroom environment engages the imaginations of children, the crises and chaos in their lives fade.

While sitting in the toddler block area last month rearranging the space, I looked over to the dramatic play area. Little Emma, having recently turned three years old, was sitting on the floor holding a bag half her size, filled with everything she could gather: plastic plates, pans, pretend food, keys, a wallet, and a phone. Usually she gleefully talks with her peers about going "bye-bye" in their imaginary travels throughout the room. This time she was sitting with a faraway look in her eyes. "Emma," I asked, "is everything OK?" "No," she said. "I miss my mommy." Her baggage was now symbolic to me of a burden she was carrying. I replied, "Your mommy loves you. She will be back soon." Then I offered her a hug, which she wholeheartedly accepted by jumping into my lap. After a few quiet moments she said, "I miss my daddy, too." I knew from my greeting time with her divorced, single mom that her dad was away this week and unable to have his visitation time with Emma. I was able to reflect that her daddy had to be away. I said, "Your daddy loves you too. I'm sure he is missing you as well." "Emma," I said, "God knows that you are feeling sad and missing your mom and dad. Would you like to pray about this?" "Yes," she replied. I then proceeded to pray in simple words, asking God to comfort Emma and to let her mommy and daddy know she was missing them very much. Then closing the prayer, I asked Emma never to forget that God wants to hear what makes her sad so that He can comfort her. With one last hug she went off, back to her imaginary world. She was carrying her bag loaded with stuff, lighter now, because we had given her burden to God.

Supporting Families

Christian early education ministry requires that teachers have a love for children and their families, and a close personal relationship with Jesus Christ. We early educators are all part of God's greater calling, which is to go out into the world and make disciples (Matthew 28:19). We need to be prayer warriors for these families. Our care needs to extend outside the classroom walls when possible and appropriate. One foster family recently received devastating news that the infant who had been in their care since birth was going to be placed with another family. We grieved with this family, praying with them and encouraging them, as they continued to come to grips with the separation. We arranged for meals to be sent home. We are to be the hands and feet of Christ in behalf of the families He brings to our classrooms. We need to take our concerns about the issues in their lives to the throne of God (1 Timothy 2:1).

We are His witnesses to His children and their families. Be generous with your smiles and encouragement, and, whenever possible, share love and kindness. Such prayers and services are the distinction of our Christian centers.

Whatever the crises the children in our centers are experiencing, we need to provide responsive, reciprocal, and respectful care that fosters in our children both the love of learning and a trust in the Lord.

REFLECTION

Just Who Is a Child's First Teacher?

By Larry Bogle. Reprinted from *CEE*, Spring 2001.

The school day is beginning, and a gaggle of children rush into the classroom, smiling and curious. "Good morning, Miss Dove!" they gush.

"Good morning, Johnny! Good morning, Celina!"

Children are acknowledging that for that day, and from their teacher, they will learn new ideas, new facts, new concepts. The teacher is the one who gives them the opportunity to learn, the one from whom they will find the answers to the mysteries in books.

Some children in Miss Dove's class are content and confident. They know they will be able to succeed in doing everything that will be expected of them that day, and they look forward to those activities. Some children are rather indifferent, knowing that they can do some of what is expected of them, but that other activities will be difficult and they will struggle. Some of those children will have already lost interest in what goes on at school. Still others are frustrated and anxious. They know that little they try to do will be completed, and that they will struggle with most of it.

This situation has been repeated since the beginning of the one-room schoolhouse with its one teacher. Does something need to change? What can be done to turn this around so that all the children who enter schools, both public and private, can perform at their optimum level?

Because America has just inaugurated a new president, education and education reform have come to the forefront of the national political agenda. Every one seems interested in reform. Yet it seems that at least two issues are missing in this scenario:

1. Too many children are not being instructed in the attitudes (including character education), habits, and skills necessary for successful social learning.
2. Too many schools aren't equipping children for lifelong learning.

Over the years, many fad ideas have been proposed at all levels, and billions of dollars have been spent on innovations. Still, few of these strategies have done much of lasting value.

Why have these ideas and expensive innovations made so little difference? Could it be that the difference between successful learners and unsuccessful ones is not so much in what we as teachers do *after* children start school as in the attitudes they bring to school?

What attitudes should children bring? Many suggest that they need confidence, motivation, effort, focus, responsibility, and perseverance. How can parents instill these qualities in their children?

Many parents and children fail to recognize that their education began long before their kindergarten and first-grade experiences—even when they were still in their mommies' tummies. Researchers and teachers are learning that from the time of conception forward, Mom's and Dad's attitudes, feelings, activities, and experiences are impacting the development of their child. However, for many parents and children, the prevalent thinking is that learning actually begins when children go to school for the first time and are introduced to books, letters, and numbers. The perception, then, is that children fail to learn because of teachers and school systems rather than parents and families.

The pattern for early childhood growth and development is set in Scripture: *And it came to pass, that, when Elisabeth heard the salutation of Mary, the babe leaped in her womb; and Elisabeth was filled with the Holy Ghost* (Luke 1:41, KJV). She told Mary, *The babe leaped in my womb for joy* (v. 44). Obviously, John was the same as other children. He experienced feelings, including joy, even before his physical birth.

Later, of Jesus' boyhood, we read: *Jesus increased in wisdom and stature, and in favour with God and man* (Luke 2:52). Jesus grew cognitively, physically, spiritually, and socially. His home with Mary and Joseph was His one-room schoolhouse, His learning center.

In two thousand years, things have not changed with children developmentally. The patterns of growth are the same (although rates are different), and parents are still the child's first teachers. As it is recognized that those formative years are critical, more and more emphasis is being given to early childhood development.

What the parents do for children in those four areas—cognitive, physical, spiritual, social—establishes the structure and framework as children mature and become what parents hope they will become. Research has given us knowledge of the nature of children and of how they learn. We understand that the family is a society in which we learn to love God, to celebrate both our likenesses and our differences, and to use cooperative and appropriate behaviors to live a socially productive life in the home setting.

In thinking about children as active learners, we as teachers have applied in our classrooms the developmental stages of Piaget and Erickson, the enhancing self-esteem model of Maslow, the moral stages of Kohlberg, and the assertive discipline strategies of Kanter. We as parents can apply many of the same concepts to the home in our child-rearing. Even instructional strategies, such as discovery learning and constructivism, can be applied at home.

How Can We Do That?

Physically, the benefits of proper food, rest, and exercise are probably the most widely known and understood of the four areas. Through various media, we are bombarded with the necessity of eating daily from the four food groups, taking vitamins, watching our fat and sugar intake, and encouraging physical activity and rest. Whether or not most parents actually promote these activities, for the most part they at least know what they should do.

9

However, in the cognitive area, there are many "teacherly" activities that parents can do to develop "thinking" skills and attitudes in children. Many of the activities use simple, at-home materials to teach profound and lifelong attitudes. For example, parents can plant seeds in a window box, water them, and watch with their children as the seeds sprout and grow into flowers or herbs. Through this activity children can learn patience, perseverance, and delayed gratification. We live in a "we want it now" generation, and we have the tools and hardware to make that want a reality. Even mechanical things such as remote controls and microwave ovens and cell telephones feed our desire for instant gratification. Is it worth while to plant a seed and wait days and weeks for it to grow and bloom? Yes! Can young children learn patience from observing that process? Yes!

Would it be helpful to give children a limited amount of TV time per week to push them into non-TV activities? "Johnny, you can have 10 hours of TV a week, max. Here is the TV schedule. Tell me which programs you want to watch in your 10 hours." This practice will teach a child not only priority-setting, but cooperation, submission to authority, focus, and even arithmetic.

What kind of teachers will these parents become?—ones who want their children to succeed and are willing to believe they can help. These parent-teachers will focus on character development, which should be an integral part of early childhood education.

In addition to character education, parents can gradually utilize techniques for teaching children cognitive skills—comprehending, reading, and writing. Piaget has taught that children develop in stages, and they will not progress to the next stage until they have successfully negotiated the stage they are in. He has taught that a child needs active learning experiences. During the earliest stage (birth through approximately two years) children are in the "sensorimotor" stage. Their work is learning about and exploring their world. Through "doing things" children discover meaning in their experiences.

In this stage children learn about themselves and the environment through motor and reflex actions. They learn that they are separate from their environment, and that aspects of their environment (parents and favorite toys) continue to exist even though they may now be outside the reach of their senses. Teaching children in this stage, then, should be geared to the sensorimotor system. Parents can modify behavior by using the senses: a frown, a stern or soothing voice—these can serve as appropriate reinforcing techniques. Parents can facilitate problem-solving strategies in very small children by doing such things as:

1. Placing the child's favorite toy on the left side one day and the right side the next day, and playing games like hide-and-seek.
2. Allowing repeated opportunities for the infant to act, using mobiles and visual displays.
3. Placing the infant in safe places where he can move freely without fear for his safety, and having different things for him to crawl on, under, over, and through.
4. Engaging her in one-on-one conversations, using turn-taking, and

responding with delight when she takes a turn.

5. Providing face-to-face interaction with finger plays, songs, books, and games like peek-a-boo.

Parents can help a toddler's throwing ability grow from simply pushing a ball on the floor to holding it on his chest and pushing it forward. Catching develops a bit later, with the first attempt consisting of closing his arms around the ball as it hits his chest. Toddlers begin to use bean-bags and smaller objects for throwing, and to play games that require some control to hit a target or drop an object into a box. They also enjoy using chalk, markers, and crayons on large boards or easels, an activity that helps them refine their coordination.

Parents need to give their children the richest variety of experiences they can manage. There must be a great deal of moving, manipulating, touching, tasting, and seeing to explore the world of color, texture, taste, sound, and movement. There should be much talking, playing repetitive games, and yes! even—especially!—reading. From the earliest days of life, both Mother and Father need to read to their child, and to read the same books over and over and over. These books will become the children's favorites, and they will want to hear them many times.

From these experiences, children will learn front-to-back orientation, top-to-bottom skills, and left-to-right reading and page order. Parents can talk to children about pictures and have them predict what will happen next. They can give children opportunities to "read" the story aloud. The children will become so proficient at this that they will parrot the words exactly and know when to turn the page!

Most importantly, children need to see parents modeling these skills. Parents who want children to be readers should read! Parents who want children to write should write! Parents should explore and comment on and converse about their world. They should be interested in all the varied experiences around them and should show these to their children.

Parents who want their children to develop morally with integrity and honesty should model integrity and honesty in even the smallest activities. Many in today's world feel we have lost our way as a nation because of the callous disregard for integrity displayed by some (even at the highest levels of government), so here is a beginning, a way for us to make a midcourse adjustment toward God's standard.

Parents want their children to grow cognitively, physically, socially, and spiritually. To promote each kind of growth, parents can and should be their children's first teachers.

REFLECTION

More than Just Words: Do Your Classrooms Reflect Your Philosophy?

By Tina Daigre. Reprinted from *CEE*, November 2005.

Two years ago a verse in Hebrews caught my attention, and I was unable to forget it. "See to it that no one misses the grace of God ..." (12:15). These words kept playing over in my mind as I thought of their implications. As a director I thought about what they meant in terms of our staff, families, children, and community. What an incredible responsibility! Fortunately, I work in a place that seeks to do just what this verse says.

Our school began years before there was even a building. It started with several visionaries who had a heart for God and for young families. These visionaries understood that a quality Christian school is more than a place for a good education; it is also a bridge to struggling, hurting families who need God. As Christian educators, we have a unique opportunity to spread God's love through the relationships we share with the children. Because their parents often look to us for support and encouragement, we have a perfect opportunity to "live Christ in front of them." To make sure we stay on course, we measure every decision we make as a school against our philosophy.

Every program has a philosophy, and we believe that it is important to be purposeful about articulating and reviewing our philosophy often to ensure that all the staff members understand it clearly. At Celebration Christian Preschool, our philosophy says that the school will "cooperate and assist parents in fulfilling their God-given responsibility" for bringing their children up in "the training and instruction of the Lord" (Ephesians 6:4).

Be Ready

One way to implement the above is to ask teachers to *be ready to pray with parents* when necessary. Sometimes as I walk through the halls of our school, I see a teacher with her arms around a parent, praying. The message is extremely powerful! It's one thing to tell parents you'll be praying for them, but it's something else entirely to say "Let's pray" and then do so. Last year, a child in our school lost his grandmother to cancer. In the weeks prior to her death, the teachers prayed with the mother and the child at different times, and they offered additional support in the final weeks. On the day of the grandmother's death, the little boy jumped up on her bed and said, "It's OK, Grandma, you can go be with Jesus now!" A few hours later she died. How powerful it was for the school and the family to share in those moments!

Also, in our lobby next to the coffee bar, we have a *prayer box* where parents can leave written prayer requests. Each morning we take the requests to our staff devotions and pray about them. We tell new families about the prayer box and encourage them to give us their requests. This year, a new family was enrolling. Before their little boy started school, we found out that his mom, who was seven months pregnant, had gone into preterm labor. Her baby was born early and weighed only a pound. Our staff had begun praying for the infant before he was born, and although we had not even met his mother, we sent her word that we were praying for the family. After the new baby had spent two months in the hospital, he was allowed to go home, where he is doing very well! That shared experience created a bond between home and school, and it gave everyone involved the blessing of watching God work. Our faith as a staff has grown tremendously as we have watched God work in our lives and in the lives of those we've prayed for!

Our teachers are also ready to offer *other kinds of assistance* in addition to prayer. Jesus shows us by example that it is best to make a quick or immediate response to a person or family in need (Matthew 8:5–13). Here are some of the many ways we stay ready:

- We keep grocery store gift cards on hand for parents experiencing financial emergencies, and we also make available free Christian financial counseling if it is needed.
- Our teachers often refer parents to our lending library for resources on such topics as discipline, marriage, and finances, and we hold monthly seminars on these topics as well.
- We have available outside resources and specialists ranging from mental health experts to speech pathologists to occupational therapists.

14

- We use the resources of our school parents to help other parents in need. This past year, a mother of two of our children underwent major back surgery and was unable to leave the hospital for six weeks. Once she could return to her home, staff members and other school parents made meals for the family for over a month! Another family said goodbye to their father, who was stationed in Iraq and would not return for more than a year. Other dads in the school signed up to offer help with mowing the lawn and meeting the occasional home maintenance need.

In our school there is now a strong sense of community, which has been created as teachers and other staff members have found opportunities to share and live out Christ's love! In order for staff members to "stand ready," they must be built up. They must be growing spiritually and be armed for the spiritual battle. In our school we require that our teachers be regular attendees of a local church. We also encourage their spiritual growth by providing a lending library of Scripture studies, including tapes, DVDs, videos, and books that specifically teach the Bible. We offer incentives to encourage completion of these studies. For every study completed, we "reward" the teachers with a gift certificate to a restaurant or store of their choice. It's important to note that the reward is not the point; rather, the point is the spiritual training and the knowledge that come from studying the Bible. We see these outcomes as important enough that we are constantly evaluating how to encourage teachers in their spiritual growth.

Commitment to Excellence

Our philosophy also says that we are committed to excellence in character development, academic achievement, and quality instruction, so it is imperative that our classroom instruction be of very high quality. Maintaining classrooms that reflect our philosophy is one of our biggest priorities. We do this in several ways:

1. We start with *teacher training*. We begin each school year with teacher orientation and training. This kind of beginning serves to remind us of why we are here and what we are striving for—children and families who know God and are growing in knowledge of Him. In our day-to-day stress and busyness, it's easy to forget how important it is to stay on course.

2. We have developed a system whereby fellow teachers and staff members can walk into a classroom at any time and do a two-to-five-minute evaluation to ensure that the classroom is functioning at a quality level. We call these "Quality Assurance Evaluations." They are short and direct, and anyone can administer them. They are tools for the teachers to use as benchmarks throughout the year.

3. Teachers are required to write a *monthly curriculum*, basing it on the age-specific objectives of their classroom. On their lesson plans teachers list the objective for each activity, ensuring that even the children's play is purposeful. For example, if a teacher lists easel painting as a daily activity, she must also list the reason doing it: for example, eye-hand coordination or crossing midline. This practice keeps the teachers in tune with the importance of their work and reminds them that there is tremendous value in what they do!

4. As a school, we recognize the God-given uniqueness of each child, so it is important that teachers *observe* children and develop curricula to fit the children's individual needs. Teachers wear aprons that hold adhesive labels. As they interact with children or even just watch them play, they can pull out an observation sticker and jot down a few notes. At the end of the day, the stickers go into each teacher's "Observation Binder," where each child has his own page. Every month these observations are analyzed to help the teacher develop specific activities that meet the needs of the children and enhance their growth.

The atmosphere of any Christian school should be different from that of a public school. And if our philosophy is *more than just words* on a sheet of paper, people will notice a difference. At the end of the day—and the school year— we hope that we as a school will be able to say that we did our best to "see to it that no one misses the grace of God."

The Power of the Christian School Community

By Julia Wurst. Reprinted from *CEE*, March 2010.

"We are keeping this family together." Those were my mom's words shortly after my dad went into prison. After he left, there was a gaping hole in our home and in our lives. Everything was about to change, and no one knew how much.

Dad left to spend 24 months in a federal prison camp during my junior year of high school. I had experienced a fairly idyllic childhood, so this circumstance came as a slap in the face. My mom would be a single mother for a while. She taught at the Christian school that my sister, Dana, my brother, Tim, and I attended. This small Christian school, Alpha Beacon, had always been a community for my family as we attended sporting events, plays, and Christmas fairs. She was working only enough to earn our tuition and a small salary, but Mom relied on her faith—and the generosity of friends—to make ends meet.

Something happened when we became a single-parent family. Some of our family stopped calling as often. People at church didn't understand what we were going through. But the faculty at Alpha Beacon wrapped their arms around us even tighter.

Emotional Protection

When a family faces a difficult circumstance, it's easy for people to see physical needs and meet them. But people in crisis need their emotional needs met as well. The staff encouraged my mom with prayer, hugs, and many lunchtimes together. Teachers took time to involve my siblings and me in activities that interested us. The school provided a safe place where we knew we wouldn't be ridiculed. My brother's class had the number of days that my dad had left in prison on the upper corner of the chalkboard. Every day, Tim's teacher would change the number so he could count down the days until his dad would be home. The whole class was able to be involved and to support Tim every day through this part of their morning routine.

Emotional protection manifests in many ways. In a true safe place, gossip and pointless talk are banned. When children hear others talking about people in negative, nonconstructive ways, they immediately sense they are not welcome. My dad committed a felony, and he was taken away from home during a pivotal time in our development. The last thing any of us needed was other people talking about our family in negative ways. The Christian school kept us safe from that.

Families That Care

A Christian school isn't just the staff; it's also the families that help make up a whole support network. One particular family "adopted" my sister. This family knew all about our dad and invested in Dana. They didn't ask her about details or her feelings. They walked with her through life. They just involved her in whatever they were doing, and she remembers them as her biggest support during that time.

"They took me in as their own," she said. "They were stability for me. They gave me a sense of normalcy. The love from [my friend's] dad always made me feel important, which was nice since my dad was gone."

The Power of Letters

One practical way to minister to prisoners is to send them letters. A few of the Alpha Beacon staff members wrote to my dad. This simple yet thoughtful gesture encouraged him and our whole family. Prisoners can struggle heavily with depression. But the more outside friends and family communicate with them, the less hopeless they feel. Reaching out to my father through words of encouragement also helped the rest of us navigate this difficult trial.

"[The letters] really kept me focused ... [and] connected," my father said. "I didn't want to be alone. My biggest fear was that I would be forgotten."

There are many ways to help families in crisis. This story is my family's journey through a complex time. We were lucky. We had an amazing support network. Many teachers and friends came alongside each of us individually, prayed with and for us, and offered themselves in unique ways.

Your preschool can be that support system for the families it serves. Listen to the Holy Spirit. Allow Him to show you the best ways to support the families in your school.

Section 1 Authors

Larry Bogle, EdD, is an adjunct professor of education at Southwestern Assemblies of God University in Waxahachie, Texas. Larry has a wide background of teaching experience that includes public school, Christian school, community college, and university teaching and administration.

Tina Daigre, BA, is the director of Celebration Christian Preschool in Brentwood, California. Tina began her career in early childhood education "playing teacher."

Carol Damschroder has served in all roles of early education for more than 25 years in Columbus, Ohio. Carol has a degree in social work from Seattle Pacific University and an additional 36 hours in early childhood development. She and her husband have three grown sons and three grandchildren.

Susannah Wayland, MEd, has a bachelor's degree in child development and elementary education. She received her master's degree in curriculum and teaching. Born and raised in Michigan, Susannah has taught in classrooms ranging from early education through fourth grade. She has two children.

Julia Wurst, BA, serves as ACSI's Media Specialist for Early Education Services. She is also the associate editor for *Christian Early Education* magazine.

Section 2:
Practical Tools

How Are We Doing?
Assessing Parent Ministry Components
By Leanne Leak

Making the Most of Parent Events

	Unexamined	Emerging	Competent	Exemplary
Maximizing Opportunities	Our parent events have not been modified in many years. There is no evaluation of effectiveness after an event.	I've noticed that some aspects of our events need to be updated. I take notes after the event so that I can put new ideas into practice next year.	I know the purpose for each parent event we sponsor, and I examine every factor to make sure we are accomplishing the purpose. If I realize that some part of the event consumes a lot of staff time and yields little benefit, it is eliminated.	I think of ways to add value to parent events. Our events strengthen families spiritually, help parents to value Christian education, and give parents something positive to talk about in the community.
Hospitality	In planning events, I don't typically consider how I can make parents feel welcome. During the event, I'm often quite busy with the logistics of the event. This tends to be my focus.	Parents are warmly greeted when they arrive at our events. If we provide refreshments, we are more concerned about functionality than presentation.	In addition to any written invitations, parents receive verbal invitations and reminders from staff. Other family members are also welcome to participate, when appropriate. In planning refreshments, we consider how to make the presentation inviting. Our attention to detail honors parents and children.	Even though our center may be large, our parent events are warmly personal as our staff have considered how to make sure no parent feels "lost in the crowd." We incorporate parents that are already involved in the center in the task of reaching out to new parents.
Working together	I've done these events for many years, so I don't need to get any ideas or assistance from parents or from my staff.	I realize that I can strengthen parent events by involving others, but I haven't determined the best ways to invite participation.	Because I know the purposes for our events, the individuals I involve have clear guidelines for participation. I am able to inspire others with the vision for the event, which gives them the desire to come alongside. I thank colaborers in the event both verbally and in writing. They have a clear sense of the worth of their contribution.	The individuals who are involved in planning and executing the event are energized by their participation. The events facilitate meaningful connections between parents and staff. In planning events, I inquire about parents' interests and needs. We respond to needs that are consistent with our mission.

23

Responding to Parents' Concerns

	Unexamined	Emerging	Competent	Exemplary
Disposition	I rehearse in my mind things that parents have said or done that annoy me. I frequently express my frustration with certain parents to other staff members. I view parents as hindrances to be avoided or overcome.	I'm aware that some parents rub me the wrong way, but try not to dwell on it. I keep my frustrations to myself. My attitude toward parents is neutral.	When I find myself at odds with individual parents, I transform my angry thoughts into prayer for the parents and situation. When I speak of parents (generally or specific individuals), I convey respect. I cultivate a biblical view of parents and honor their God-given role in the child's life.	I embrace the privilege of regularly praying for parents. My comments about parents indicate that I believe the best about their motives and their potential. I receive parents as gifts to our center, knowing we will be strengthened by their input and be better for being held accountable.
Listening	When parents bring their concerns, I am anxious for them to finish, so I can explain my point of view.	I listen to parents and wait until they have fully expressed their concerns before replying. My response directly acknowledges their concerns.	Before responding to parents, I ask clarifying questions and make sure I truly understand the facts of their concern, as well as the feelings triggered by the situation.	I am not afraid of periods of silence and allow parents plenty of time to express their thoughts. I am aware of my own body language and tone of voice and regulate my response to help parents feel comfortable expressing concerns.
Mutually Acceptable Solutions	If one of our policies or procedures isn't working for a child, the parent must have inappropriate expectations.	Everything that is done at our center has a reason behind it.	Even though I can explain the principles behind our policies, I'm open to parents' suggestions and know which procedures are simply preferences.	I collaborate with parents to solve problems so that the child's needs are met without compromising our foundational principles.
Building Bridges	When I sense a parent has a problem with something in our center, I wait to see if it will blow over before initiating a conversation.	I establish a positive relationship with parents early in the year and encourage my teachers to do the same.	After I successfully resolve a problem with a parent, I follow up with a written note or phone call, expressing appreciation for the parents' willingness to work through a difficult situation.	We've established strategies to elicit feedback from parents (suggestion box, parent surveys, etc.) so that we can proactively respond before a small problem becomes a large one.

Cultivating Relationships with Parents

	Unexamined	Emerging	Competent	Exemplary
Initiating	I wait for parents to come to me. It's not my responsibility to seek to develop a relationship with them.	I make sure that I am visible in the center, especially at strategic times like drop-off and pick-up. Parents know my name and my face. I am perceived as friendly.	I endeavor to know the names of the parents in my school, if this is feasible. (*If my school is very large, the entire administrative team makes an effort in this area.*) I can read parents and am sensitive to their desire for interaction. They can tell from my words and my body language that I am available and interested, but my inquiries are never intrusive.	Our entire staff is proactive and intentional about initiating relationships with parents. We pray for parents regularly. We are alert to parents' nonverbal signals that they are experiencing difficulty, and we offer support and prayer.
Fragrance	As a director, I have a lot of responsibilities and a lot on my mind. Because I'm so focused on these tasks, some parents may not see me as approachable. I am sometimes described as gruff, but once parents get to know me they realize I don't mean any offense by my sharp comments.	I realize that my appearance and my countenance contribute to the welcoming culture of our center.	Parents are drawn to me and to my staff because they can tell that we care about them and their children. We seek to make God's love visible through our words and actions, becoming vessels through which the kindness of God may draw people to Jesus.	Everyone at our center recognizes the necessity of cultivating an inner beauty. We are graced with gentle and quiet spirits (I Peter 3:4) that are Christ-honoring and attractive.
Collaborating	I have many years experience leading an early education center. Because of this, I know what's best for all children. Parents have a lot to learn from me.	I listen to parents' ideas as well as sharing my own perspective with them. I realize that parents have insight into their own children that we need to hear. Although we have limited opportunities for parent involvement, we are pleased if it is offered.	I recognize that parents have a variety of backgrounds and experiences that can enrich our classrooms and our center. I creatively discover ways to involve parents that enhance our program and help us achieve our mission.	When parents are involved in classrooms they are given clear, written instructions for successful participation. We orient parents to our philosophy and core values to minimize misunderstanding and conflict.

25

Effective Parent Conferences

	Unexamined	Emerging	Competent	Exemplary
Preparation	My teachers are sensible people, and they have good memories. They need little preparation for parent conferences and don't require support or training from me.	My teachers prepare for parent conferences, and both the teachers and the parents benefit from this preparation. If teachers ask, I'll give them advice, but I haven't developed guidelines that address our school's expectations for how parent conferences are conducted.	We have established goals for parent conferences, and our teachers know what we want to see accomplished. I provide support to all my teachers and training to teachers who are new to our school or to the field. My teachers recognize that prayer is a significant part of their preparation.	Teachers collaborate in conference preparation with other teachers or aides who also work with the child. I pray with teachers who feel anxious about conducting parent conferences. Teachers have an opportunity to talk with me or with each other about what they learned and what they might want to do differently in the future.
Communication	My teachers don't worry about the impact of their words. Parents can handle the truth about their child. We aren't concerned about tact or separating facts about the child from our opinions.	I talk with my staff about how to communicate difficult information. My teachers are able to put themselves in a parent's place and understand the power of their words to build up or tear down. My teachers take advantage of opportunities to pray with parents at the beginning or end of a conference.	My teachers cultivate empathy for parents and compassion for children that enables them to engage in difficult conversations about children's development with graciousness. My teachers realize that withholding truthful information about a child is not a loving action. They seek to make these conversations productive by developing a positive relationship with parents early in the school year.	My teachers realize that parents' responses to difficult news may not be positive. They seek to maintain an open relationship, knowing that parents may be more open to dialogue after they have time to think through the issues.
Parent Involvement	Our conferences are an opportunity for parents to find out what we know about their child. They will learn a lot from listening to us.	My teachers realize that they can learn about the child by listening to the parent. If a parent volunteers information about their child, it is received, but we do not actively seek this.	My teachers involve parents as partners by finding out about their goals for their child and listening to parents' insights as a way to better serve the family.	Teachers elicit information from parents prior to the conference, so they are prepared to respond to parents' requests for information in specific areas.

Transforming Parent Education

	Unexamined	Emerging	Competent	Exemplary
Parental Responsibility	I know that Scripture speaks to the parents' responsibility for their child's education and spiritual formation, but our center has not taken any responsibility for conveying this truth to parents.	Because we want to support parents in their biblical role, we are available to answer their questions and give them resources if they ask us. We don't yet have a plan for training and equipping parents to be successful in raising godly children.	As a school, we recognize that our impact on children's lives is limited unless we equip parents. We offer parents support for raising godly children through various methods. We have articulated our beliefs in this area so that we have a clear statement of parental responsibility that leaves no doubt about our biblical position on this topic.	We regularly evaluate our efforts for supporting parents, and we make adjustments to our programs to make them more effective. We help parents to connect with other parents so that they have peer support and an opportunity to see biblical parenting modeled in daily life.
Biblical Teaching	We offer parent education opportunities that we think will appeal to parents. We don't particularly consider whether our training will help parents with their child's spiritual formation.	We are beginning to consider how we can help parents teach their children biblical truth and influence their child's spiritual formation. We realize that we first need to refine our school's efforts in these areas and then plan to turn our focus to equipping parents.	We are able to explain to parents the strategies our school is using to encourage children's spiritual development. We have developed a plan for cultivating parents' interest in this area and providing ongoing training for parents.	In developing avenues for equipping parents to guide their child's spiritual formation, we have considered the differing needs of believing parents and parents who are not yet followers of Christ. Our teachers capitalize on opportunities to influence and support parents through informal interactions, as well as through our planned trainings.
Developmental Process	Although our teachers understand child development and our program is designed to support children's development, we assume parents will learn about these things by observing how we teach their child.	When parents ask, our teachers can explain how children grow and learn and why we teach the way we do. We don't have a plan for formally sharing this information with parents.	We provide written materials and interactive trainings that inform parents. We give parents specific ideas for activities they can do at home that enhance children's development and strengthen the parent-child relationship.	As a result of our training and supportive materials, parents gain confidence. We assess our written materials to eliminate jargon and to make sure the information is accessible to parents.

27

I want to grow in this (these) parent ministry component(s):

These are some steps I can take to expand my skills in this area (*check all that apply*):

☐ Talk with other directors who are strong in this area.

☐ Read professional material on this topic.

☐ Study relevant passages of Scripture.

☐ Spend a period of time seeking insight in prayer (alone or with a partner).

☐ Other: _____

Whom can I share my commitment with?

When would I like them to check back with me so I can share my progress?

REFLECTION

The Family Connection

By D'Arcy Maher. Reprinted from *CEE*, December 2010.

Since parents are a child's primary teacher, schools/programs must respect the critical role parents play in supporting the growth and development of their child.... Effective partnerships with parents are a vital part of quality education. Between staff and parents, a rapport is built that supports communication between the home and the education program.... The staff actively initiates relationships with families, cultivating communication and providing multiple avenues for ongoing parent involvement and feedback. (ACSI 2008, 11)

Emerging Practice—The practice may be inconsistently implemented, but the teacher is committed to learning and growing in this area; program and staff-member practices show awareness but have incomplete policies or expectations.

Consistent Implementation—Program and staff-member practices express care, concern, and understanding of family dynamics and needs.

Exemplary Performance—Program and staff-member practices have been thoughtfully and intentionally determined. Among the staff, there is a culture of accountability for ministry to families and a deep respect for parents and caregivers of enrolled children.

Valuing a Child's Family Culture

Emerging Practice	Consistent Implementation	Exemplary Performance
Children have a chance to share about their family culture as part of a thematic unit.	Children are consistently viewed in the context of their family's culture. Staff members are sensitive to culture, and they seek out ways to further understand the cultures represented in their classroom.	Cultural awareness permeates the program, from the materials in the learning centers, the snacks provided, and the children's literature selected, to the activities planned. Staff members regularly embrace opportunities to celebrate the beauty and diversity of the humanity created in God's image.

Understanding Changing Family Units

Emerging Practice	Consistent Implementation	Exemplary Performance
Program practices anecdotally accommodate significant changes in family units. Staff members discuss changes in family structures in order to solve a specific problem.	Program leaders aggressively seek to understand the obvious and subtle changes of the audience they serve and to respond significantly to families' needs. Staff members participate in brainstorming to serve the needs of the families enrolled.	Program leaders invest time to understand, track, solicit feedback from, and become experts on the families they serve. They find ways to accommodate language and economic barriers and cultural differences. Staff members are specifically trained to serve the needs of children and families.

Inviting Parents and Guardians Into Daily Routines

Emerging Practice	Consistent Implementation	Exemplary Performance
Parents and guardians are warmly greeted in the program. They are welcome and expected guests at special events.	During the enrollment process, parents and guardians receive a list of participation opportunities. Teachers invite parents to and remind them about opportunities and accommodate parental involvement.	Program leaders establish classroom schedules and routines with parent involvement in mind. They match parents' and guardians' interests to participation opportunities and create tailored interactions. The program provides orientation for parental involvement. Parents' ideas are cultivated and implemented (as appropriate) in the classrooms. Parents spontaneously comment that they feel like valued partners in their children's education.

Providing Clear Communication on Children's Progress

Emerging Practice	Consistent Implementation	Exemplary Performance
Communicating a child's progress is generally confined to brief conversations during drop-off or pickup, which—though warm, friendly, and respectful—tend to focus on health, safety, and behavioral issues. Occasionally, impressions about physical, cognitive, social/emotional, or spiritual development are shared.	Parents are invited to participate in setting goals for their children when they are introduced to a new classroom. Teachers are trained to recognize progress indicators. They collect multiple means of documentation on progress. Personal conferences are scheduled; the child's progress in each developmental domain is discussed.	Staff members receive extensive training on observing and recording children's progress and on conducting parent conferences. Parents receive multiple opportunities to participate in nurturing their child's progress, and their observations are discussed and valued.

Reference

ACSI. 2008. *REACH: Accreditation manual for EE–12 North American and international schools.* Colorado Springs, CO: Association of Christian Schools International.

Where do you land on this rubric?

What areas do you need to grow in?

What areas of strength do you need to share with other educators?

What categories would you add to this chart? What ratings would you provide?

What are your goals in working with parents this year?

REFLECTION

Informing Parents About Teaching Through Experiences

By D'Arcy Maher. Reprinted from *CEE*, Winter 2004.

The Million-Dollar Question

"I understand that children learn through experiences, but how do I convince parents that children don't need workbooks to learn?" Does that question sound familiar? Have you asked it yourself? What do you tell parents who feel that children are not accomplishing anything if there aren't any workbook pages in the weekly folder?

Experiences, Experiences, Experiences

In *Child-Sensitive Teaching*, Karyn Henley provides an excellent example of learning through experiences: "Learning occurs when experience touches truth. Mommy says, 'Keep your hand away from the oven door. The oven gets hot.' That is a truth. What happens when the child touches the oven door? He has an experience. He learns a truth: the oven gets hot" (2002, 83).

Henley further explains, "What is an experience? Experience is something that happens to us involving our senses: sight, hearing, smell, taste, touch. The more of the five senses that are involved, the stronger the experience will be, and the stronger the memory of it will be" (84). But while parents may give mental assent to the importance of experiences, you can provide an activity for them in order to drive home this point.

Parents Engaged as Learners

Plan a three-part activity and invite parents and children to a night of fun. Parents and children sit together at round tables that are preferably child sized. In the middle of the table, place a piece of fruit (pineapples and peaches work great for this activity), paper plates, and a knife for cutting. Instruct a child at each table to investigate the fruit and pass it around—encourage smelling too! Begin a list titled

Real Pineapple and ask for volunteers to tell you all they can about the fruit; the list can be on a flip chart, an overhead projector, or a PowerPoint program. Now invite a parent to slice the fruit and pass it around for everyone to taste. After everyone enjoys a bite, ask for volunteers to tell you everything about what they just tasted. Add all comments to the original list; the list will probably be quite long.

After cleaning up all the plates, napkins, and silverware from the activity, distribute a plastic version of the fruit used in the previous experience. Ask for the plastic fruit to be passed around the tables, begin a new list titled Plastic Pineapple, and ask volunteers to share observations of the plastic fruit. When the responses slow, it's time to begin the final part of the activity. Collect the plastic fruit and distribute a coloring sheet of the same fruit used in the previous two activities. Allow time for everyone to color the picture. Begin another list titled Pineapple Coloring Sheet and ask volunteers to share things about the coloring sheet.

Now it's time to compare the three lists. The list titled Real Pineapple will be the longest. The activity prepares parents to hear your philosophy, which may include these points:

34

1. Children engage at a higher level when involved in an activity.
2. The learning that results from an activity cannot be replicated with a coloring sheet or workbook.
3. The best way to monitor a child's learning is simply to ask questions about classroom happenings. Parents can read the classroom newsletter and review the posted lesson plans. You can assist them in preparing questions to encourage their child to share about learning activities.
4. When children miss a day of class, a simple workbook page does not capture the level of experiential learning that takes place in the classroom.

Parent Activity: Take Two

Another way to provide parents an opportunity to experience your philosophy would be to set up something similar with a classroom pet, such as a guinea pig or a stuffed animal, and then with a coloring picture of the pet. Explain how the ongoing training of responsibility is woven throughout the curriculum when the children care for a classroom pet over the course of the year.

Favorite Quotations

Listed below are my favorite quotations, which you may want to sprinkle throughout your parent activity:

We create experiences to which we link the truth we want to teach. These experiences are called activities. We teach toward the experience children have during the activities. (Henley 2002, 87)

Preschoolers are perpetual learners. They are active, involved learners, propelled by a desire for discovery. They learn by examining, exploring, experimenting. They learn what they are ready to learn and discard or disregard what is beyond their grasp. They do not respond well to forced learning. But when readiness for learning certain concepts or skills exists, preschoolers pursue an activity or experience with persistence. (Carey and Henry 1988, 22)

Learning is forestalled when enjoyment is not present for a child. A preschooler needs to experience joy and delight in an activity for optimum learning to occur. (Carey and Henry 1988, 23)

References

Carey, Geraldine Addison, and Kay Vandevier Henry. 1988. *Teaching in church weekday education*. Nashville, TN: Convention Press.

Henley, Karyn. 2002. *Child-sensitive teaching*. Rev. ed. Nashville, TN: Child Sensitive Communication, LLC.

REFLECTION

REFLECTION

The Message Was Sinking In

By Jim Ed Hardaway. Reprinted from *CEE*, May 2006.

My five-year-old son, Carson, lives in a world of his own. The complexity of life goes no further than the battle of good and evil between the two action figures he holds in his hands. No big decisions to make, no bills to pay, no heavy responsibilities to fulfill—besides the orders from his mother to clean his room—that is, until he starts kindergarten in the fall.

Until then, he's a kid, and being a kid requires no binding prequalification; he is free to imagine without having to impress others around him. Sometimes I sit back and watch him play, and I'm amazed at his creativity and outlook on life. He's not just living; he's alive—alive with energy, alive with character, and alive with laughter.

One of his favorite things to say to me, after doing something silly, is, "Was that funny, Dad?" Everything about him encompasses what a five-year old boy was created to be—playful, energetic, and inquisitive.

Can he balance a checkbook? Can he manage a corporation? No. It's hard enough for him to complete the task of cleaning his room. Actually, he could if he asserted a little more willpower. Speaking of power of will, can he know God? I mean, can he really understand God's existence or comprehend the validity of the gospel? The answer is yes! In fact, he came to me the other night and asked me to help him write his first song. On a small sticky note, with pencil in hand, I wrote down the words as he gave them to me:

Life of the Lord
The Lord is the best
The Lord is cool
The Lord is fun with Jesus
Jesus is God too
He made the earth
He made light

Afterward, Carson and his older brother, Caleb, performed the song for me, complete with a hip-hop groove and a few dance moves. It's not very long, it doesn't rhyme, and it probably won't win a GRAMMY award. But it came from the heart of Carson, and it speaks volumes about his knowledge of the Father. And hey, there's even some sound theology in those lines! Don't forget, he's only five.

I grew up as a preacher's kid on the Gulf Coast of south Texas, and I can't remember a Sunday morning when I wasn't at church. My dad was a faithful Southern Baptist minister, and my mom an avid woman of the Word. I even remember the little plastic loaf of bread that held Scripture cards on the center of our dining-room table. We read one of the cards every morning.

When I was Carson's age, my church experience was more than wonderful. If I wasn't sleeping on the pews, I was crawling around underneath them with my own set of action figures in hand, or sometimes Hot Wheels cars. But I was still listening.

And yes, I was the kid who was never late for Sunday school, and it was fine with me. Every week promised a smashing new Bible lesson with the cut out paper Jesus on the flannel board. It was always fun to turn Him upside down when the teacher wasn't looking. **The message was getting across even if Jesus was doing a handstand throughout the entire lesson.**

Although I don't recall the titles of the sermons, or even the reasons why my mother had to give me the stiletto elbow on many occasions to refocus my attention, the message was sinking in. My parents' testimony was being lived out before me, and the fact that I was a sinner in need of a Savior was very clear. Of course, the extent of my sin life involved writing on the bathroom walls with crayons and taking a handful of the Lord's Supper wafers instead of just one.

My salvation experience happened one weekend in the fall of 1975 when my parents left me at a friends' home for an overnight stay. On that Saturday morning I sat on the couch in my pajamas, watching *Fat Albert and the Cosby Kids*. It was one of my favorite cartoons. In that moment I felt the Spirit of God calling me, and my life was about to change forever. I got up, went to the back bedroom, and got down on my knees next to the bunk bed I had slept in the night before. I asked Jesus into my heart at four-and-a-half years of age. The message was too compelling for me to ignore any longer.

There's such a valuable lesson for us as adults to learn here. How many times have we written off children for not knowing anything, or ignored them because they were *just children* or even *in the way*. After all, they're just playing, not listening. In fact, aren't they too young to understand? Jesus had something to say about that.

In Mark 10:13–16, we read about a group of children who gathered around Jesus. They were quickly rebuked by the disciples, who in a feeble effort attempted to remove them so that Jesus could attend to more important things. *The Message* (Peterson 2002) reads, "The people brought children to Jesus, hoping he might touch them. The disciples shooed them off. But Jesus was irate and let them know it: 'Don't push these children away. Don't ever get between them and me. These children are at the very center of life in the kingdom. Mark this: Unless you accept God's kingdom in the simplicity of a child, you'll never get in.' Then, gathering the children up in his arms, he laid his hands of blessing on them."

In another passage, Matthew 18:2–4, He even tells us that He wants us to change and become like children. He suggests that they are "the greatest in the kingdom of heaven" (v. 4)! Why would He say that? Most of us are mistaken in thinking that God is somehow impressed with our spiritual maturity. In reality, our so-called maturity has often kept us from some of His greatest blessings.

Through these examples I've mentioned, we discover this simple truth about children: they're willing to abandon who they are to go to God for who He is! Carson is not just a child; he is the model of everything that God wants me to be. **A child models everything we need to receive Christ fully.** Acceptance—they are usually willing to forgive without holding petty grudges. Humility—their lives aren't barracked with walls of pride that get in the way. Zeal—their energy and ability to conquer boredom is remarkable, and they don't rely on the latest trends to fuel their attitudes toward God.

So the next time you see a kid climbing a tree in your neighborhood, the next time your students decide to investigate belly buttons during the Bible story, the next time you see a group of preschoolers on a playground, or the next time you look into the eyes of your very own kid, remember, they're *not just children*. They're who you need to become like to capture the heart of God.

Reference
Peterson, Eugene H. 2002. *The message: The Bible in contemporary language.* Colorado Springs, CO: NavPress.

REFLECTION

The Virtue Tree:
Shaping Children as Moral Doers

By Teena Ingram. Reprinted from *CEE*, Spring 2005.

One preschooler's mother shocked me into action with her story. I had been teaching on the Fruit of the Spirit, using stories and songs with the children in our preschool. Things seemed to be going well; the children enjoyed the stories and sang like a choir of angels. Then a mother told us about an event at her home.

At preschool, four-year-old Sara had learned the song called "Gentleness." Her mother was moved by the words of the song and by how well Sara sang it. She asked Sara if she could videotape Sara singing the song and send the tape to Grandmother. Sara's mother also wanted the younger sister to be in the tape so that Grandmother could see both of them. Sara stood up tall next to her little sister and began singing the song softly and with much feeling:

> Gentleness, gentleness,
> You show me Your gentleness.
> How I love You!

Her little sister didn't know the song but got caught up in the moment. She began to sing along, out of tune and with the wrong words. Sara abruptly stopped the song, turned to her sister, slapped her on the cheek, and snarled, "You can't sing with me—you don't even know the song!" Then Sara turned sweetly to the camera and continued the song.

The lesson was clear: stories and songs alone will not lead to the out-working of virtues in a child's life. While they both instruct, they will not bridge that gap between *hearing* and *doing*.

Since that day, we at the school have found ways to bridge the gap. Our program integrates morality and virtues throughout the day and throughout the curriculum. The instruction does not stand alone as a special unit or focus. Children see what virtues look like in a four-year-old and in a typical four-year-old's day. They take home the ability to make moral decisions at bedtime, at mealtime, and in public. At preschool they apply their moral learning during circle time, snack time, rest time, and free play with friends.

We call our program "The Virtue Tree." In our covered entry area near the front door stands the four-foot-tall virtue tree. Its barren branches gradually fill during the week with virtue slips that recognize instances when children display good moral choices. In this way, virtues are emphasized, and parents are drawn into the process.

Here is how the tree grows in beauty:

1. Each month we select a virtue for concentrated training. While social norms and courtesies are important, we focus on biblical qualities that please God. Some examples are compassion, caring, consideration, co-operation, courtesy, diligence, friendliness, generosity, gentleness, help-fulness, joyfulness, kindness, patience, perseverance, respect, responsibility, self-control, thankfulness, and trustworthiness. Often the virtue we emphasize follows our monthly Bible theme. Sometimes we choose one that we think the children need to learn *now*! One or two months out of the year we broaden the focus to review all virtues.

2. We choose a Bible verse or a simple phrase to emphasize the virtue. We recite the verse or phrase each morning. To help the children memorize, we use catchy piggyback songs and easy hand motions, keeping the verse or phrase short.

3. As teachers, we pay special attention to our own behaviors so that children see the virtue being modeled. We are still growing, so this attention has not hurt any of us!

4. A supportive curriculum expands the children's understanding of the virtue. Books selected for their emphasis of the virtue stimulate discussions of moral choices in life situations, and role-playing using staff or children provides practice in choosing rightly.

5. Throughout the day, the children receive virtue slips for displaying the virtue of the month. A little basket contains blank slips and an assortment of colored permanent markers. When the class goes outside, the basket goes too. Next to the basket is a clear plastic container with an easy-

to-pop top. We have used large, attractive, colorful letters to label this container the "virtue jar." When teachers see a child displaying the virtue of the month, they take a virtue slip out of the basket and write a short description of what the child did, while the child watches. The child then puts the slip in the jar. An example for the virtue of helping is, "Taylor moved the step stool close to the sink so that Shane could stand on it to wash his hands."

6. At the end of the day before the children leave, we take all the virtue slips from the jar and read them aloud. This process recognizes children for excellence in virtue and helps all the children understand how to apply that virtue in everyday life.

7. At the end of each day, we affix the virtue slips to the virtue tree by sliding them into slits on the branches. Arriving and departing parents and children watch the tree grow in beauty over the week.

8. On Fridays we remove the virtue slips and put them in the children's cubbies to be taken home.

Experience has taught us these hints to make the program go well:

- If we know children are doing something *just to be seen*, we tell them we will wait and "catch" them when they don't know we're watching.

- Teachers and children can report a virtue they notice in someone else, *but* children may not report what they themselves have done.

- We keep track of the children whose names have been put in the jar to make sure all the children experience success. Ironically, the particularly challenging children tend to have their name in the jar most often. Because it is so encouraging for teachers to see these children succeed, we tend to "catch" them more readily.

- We ask parents to take the slips home at the end of the week instead of at the end of each day.

- We change the design of the virtue slips monthly to fit the weather, seasons, or holidays throughout the year. Some of the designs we use are fall leaves, acorns, snowflakes, hearts, large buds and blossoms, apples, butterflies, raindrops, birds, and Christmas ornaments.

Parents share the teachers' joy at seeing lives changed. Because parents are excited about this program's success, they have begun making their own virtue slips at home to extend what their children are learning at school. Parents post the slips from school and from home all over the children's walls, on refrigerators, and even on windows of homes. Virtue slips are beginning to capture display space from the ever-popular artwork!

REFLECTION

Home Visits: Why Do Them?

By Becky Lockwood. Reprinted from *CEE*, September 2006.

Have you been at the end of your rope with one specific child? Have you tried everything, and nothing seems to work? Have you tried visiting that child's home? I, like my coworkers, wasn't convinced that a home visit would change anything. I weighed the pros and cons. There were only two negatives. The first was the time that it was going to take, and the second was the emotional pain that I would experience because of the children who had less-than-appealing home lives.

Getting Started

"Home and school are a young child's two most important worlds. Children must bridge these two worlds every day. If home and school are connected in positive and respectful ways, children feel secure" (Dodge, Colker, and Heroman 2002, 211). By visiting the homes of the children in my class, I gained a tremendous insight into their world. I was able to meet the children and their family members on safe ground. A teacher is much less threatening in the family's territory. The family has control of the situation. The children have the opportunity to see you outside the classroom. They realize that you are a real person and that you do everyday tasks outside school. They also realize that you genuinely care about them. The parents gain a sense of comfort with you and see that you are interested in their child. It is important to keep in mind that you "go with the intention of getting to know each family member and building a relationship, not judging" (217).

The Agenda

I generally schedule my home visits to take place after school during the week. I post my schedule on my board outside the classroom. It clearly defines the time that I am available, and I allow for flexibility in my schedule. I post varying times and days of the week. I also state the amount of time I will be there. At times I have been invited to dinner. Whether you have dinner with a family is strictly your personal preference. You as a teacher set the parameters of the visit.

45

When I arrive, I give the child a gift. It is something very simple such as a book or coloring book that I can read or work on while I am there. When I leave, the child has something that is a reminder of my visit. The agenda of my typical visit is as follows:

4:00 PM: Arrive. Briefly visit with each person. This may be the first time to meet one of the parents or any siblings.

4:10 PM: Tour the house. Focus on the child's room.

4:15 PM: Play a game, read a book, or color a picture.

4:30 PM: Express gratitude for the visit, and make your way out. Remind the child to tell all his friends about the visit. When he does, the other children get excited!

If you do not think you will be able to visit all the children in your class, begin with the hard-to-reach children or parents first. You will benefit most from those visits. You can schedule them with events such as illness, the birth of a sibling, or a family crisis. Observe **everything** around you. You will gain so much insight into children just by spending time with them! Take special notice of the following:

- Are the walls decorated?
- Is there noise around the house?
- What does the child's room look like?
- How do the parents interact with the children? Do they talk at them or with them?
- Are there noticeable rules in place?
- Does the child have any responsibilities?
- Is the house tidy?
- What is the child's favorite thing to do at home?
- How does the child act at home with the parents? (Remember that the child will be excited to see you.)

What You Have to Gain

Still not sold? Let me tell you about my first home visit. In my class, I had a child I could not get through to. I talked and talked and talked with this child and her parents. My director asked me how I felt about visiting her house. By that time, I was willing to do anything! I was utterly amazed when I arrived. The front yard was littered with toys and bikes (keep in mind that the house was in a very nice neighborhood). I went inside and noticed that the house smelled dirty. The kitchen was piled with dirty dishes, and groceries were sitting on the counter. I also noticed that this family of five had a table with only three chairs. I had visited for a few minutes when my little friend wanted to show me some pictures. They were from her birth. There weren't any recent pictures. We took a tour of the house. Wow! Again I was in shock. There weren't any sheets on any beds, and there were no play things in her room. There was one very dirty bathroom, and there were remnants of a pillow that had been torn up by the family dog. I had an "aha!" moment. How could I expect this child to have any sense of pride or self-respect when she lived in such an environment? I left that visit more determined than ever to reach that child. What I viewed as the last straw ended up being the first. That child and I bonded that day. I made a connection with that child's parents that day as well.

After the visit, the child was no longer tardy. She was prepared for class, and she had a new bounce in her step. She realized that I *cared*! I cried many tears over that sweet child. Today, she is successful in kindergarten. I still go to her house, a new house with sheets on the beds, decorations, and a clean smell. I still join her and her family for dinner when they celebrate a success. I am also consulted by the parents when they have issues. What a bond was formed from just one small visit that said, "You are important," and "I value you as a member of my class."

Bring the Information Back to the Classroom

There are several ways in the classroom to spotlight your home visits. I use the information I gain as casual conversation during informal times. When we gather at the lunch table, I might inquire how the child's pet is or what a sibling is doing. Asking questions strengthens the bond with that child while at the same time builds excitement in another child who hears your questions. There are many ways to bring the information back to the classroom. The most important thing to consider is what works best for you and your environment. Remember, "It begins now, here, and with you! It begins with the very next child God brings across your path. Every child you encounter is a divine appointment. With each one you have the power and opportunity to build the child up or tear the child down" (Stafford 2005, 9).

In Closing

I now make it my goal to visit each child in my class at least one time during the year. Are you still not convinced? I challenge you to try the home visit with your most at-risk student. You are sure to glean a bit of information that will be helpful to you. It takes only 30 minutes. It could change that child for the rest of the year.

References

Dodge, Diane Trister, Laura J. Colker, and Cate Heroman. 2002. *The creative curriculum for preschool*. 4th ed. Washington, DC: Teaching Strategies.

Stafford, Wess. 2005. *To small to ignore: Why children are the next big thing*. Colorado Springs, CO: WaterBrook Press.

REFLECTION

"Mommy Come Get Me?"

By Paula Cowart. Reprinted from *CEE*, Spring 2004.

"Mommy come get me?" Victoria asked for the umpteenth time that day. While Miss Natalie, Victoria's teacher, knelt to reassure her that her mother would indeed come to get her at the end of the preschool day, she could not help wondering whether Victoria would ever become comfortable with preschool. Each day Victoria cried when her mother left and periodically asked where her mother was and when she would come back. Although she seemed to have a good time playing with her new friends and participating in learning activities, her tears were often close to the surface and ready to flow as she asked the familiar question, "Mommy come get me?"

Transition, whether it is moving from one bedroom to another, accepting a new family member, or going to a new preschool class, can be hard to handle. Preschoolers thrive on continuity and routine. They find great security in knowing what to expect and who will be involved. However, as parents and teachers, we know that change is inevitable, and we must learn how to help our preschoolers deal with it. In the book *Developmentally Appropriate Practice in Early Childhood Programs*, Sue Bredekamp and Carol Copple underscore the importance of handling transitions properly as they remind us that "transitions can create discontinuity or contribute to development, depending on what adults do to help children" (1997, 121).

How do parents and teachers work together to make transitions a positive developmental step? The first and most important step is to communicate. Parents must have positive discussions with their child about the upcoming change. In the case of starting preschool, a child who has not previously been in group settings may have an especially difficult time dealing with the transition to preschool. Because parents know more about their child than anyone else does, they can take advantage of their child's existing preferences to paint a positive picture of preschool. When a child is playing dress-up at home, the parent can remind her that there will be dress-up clothes at preschool. Parents can drive by the preschool occasionally and point it out to their child, reminding the child how much fun preschool will be.

This concept can be adapted for other situations as well. If a new baby is coming, parents can start talking with the preschooler about such topics as when the baby will arrive, where it will sleep, and what some possible names are. In the case of a new baby, parents often wonder, "When do we tell the older child?" It is usually best for parents to mention it to the preschooler as soon as they begin to tell others, without focusing on the subject too much until a month or so before the baby is expected to arrive.

The second step in making transitions a positive developmental step is to build familiarity. Preschoolers, as well as adults, like to know what to expect in a new situation. Expectant parents can visit other families with babies to help their preschooler get accustomed to being around infants. If moving to a new house is on the horizon, parents can take their preschooler by the house as often as possible to explore the new surroundings. Most preschools allow prospective families to visit classrooms in order to help the parent and child get a feel for the preschool climate and routines. Ideally, the families visit during a regular school day when typical activities are taking place. At Little Learners Preschool, we operate only during the school year, so we have an open house a week or so before school begins each fall. The teachers have their rooms ready for school, and parents drop in with their preschoolers to spend between 10 and 30 minutes in the room together. The children explore the centers, play with toys, and interact with the teachers while the parent is present to introduce, interpret, and encourage. Parents then have a reference point for discussion about preschool with their child for the next week or so before the school year begins. We encourage parents to talk about what the child saw and enjoyed at preschool and to remind the child that he will get to return soon and have a great time playing with his new friends while Mom does other things.

For many parents and teachers, the third step is the hardest. It is the act of calm acceptance. Loving adults do not want to see children upset. Parents and teachers do everything that they can to avoid distress for a child and to resolve a dilemma when it occurs. However, in the types of transitions addressed in this article, some tears and fears are a definite possibility and often a probability, depending on the child's personality. Victoria, the child described at the beginning of this article, did cry off and on for the first two months of school. Her mom knew that preschool would be a good experience for Victoria, who had never been in a group situation before, and was therefore determined to make it work. She walked Victoria to the classroom door each day, kissed her goodbye, and smilingly told her that she would be back in the afternoon. It was probably one of the most difficult things she ever did. The teachers took Victoria into the room, helped her get involved in an activity, and reassured her that Mommy would, indeed, come back to get her. Eventually, with much love and support from all the adults in her life, Victoria adjusted to preschool and now enters her classroom each day with a smile, ready to explore new worlds.

The writer of Ecclesiastes reminds us that "there is a time for everything" (Ecclesiastes 3:1, NLT). Let us embrace change with our preschoolers as we lovingly prepare them to grow and develop into the emotionally solid, confident children God has called them to be.

Reference

Bredekamp, Sue, and Carol Copple, eds. 1997. *Developmentally appropriate practice in early childhood programs*. Washington, DC: National Association for the Education of Young Children.

REFLECTION

REFLECTION

Active Dads = Increased Investment

By Darlene Buchanan Bladon. Reprinted from *CEE*, March 2007.

Only 80 children attend our small preschool. As I am sure you are aware, the attendance at parent meetings in most schools is typically low. Each year I seek the Lord for new ideas, concepts, and inventions for our preschool, and I had determined that for the 2005/2006 school year I would do something to increase parent meeting participation.

So during my prayer time I asked for a truly interesting and different way to increase participation in parent meetings. Somewhere around one-third of our parents, mostly mothers, make up a core group that attends everything. This amount of participation is not the vision of the preschool at all, and many times I have become discouraged and weary about the lack of attendance and enthusiasm, especially from fathers.

During the first parent meeting of the year, the Lord gave me an idea. I noticed that the moms had plenty to say and that the dads were quiet. On many of the dads' faces I also saw a desire to speak, but their reluctance was clearly visible. So the thought came to me, "Split them up, create a setting where they may freely speak their hearts, and see what happens."

I chose to facilitate the moms' meetings with a cofacilitator who is both a mother of three young children and our preschool teacher. I wanted the parents and grandparents to feel they had someone who could relate to them about their issues. For the men I chose two generations of men: a grandfather, who is a member of the church's Men's Fellowship Board, and his son, who had an elementary-age child and an infant at the time. The meetings took place from 4 to 6 PM a day apart: moms on Tuesday and dads on Wednesday of the same week every other month. In a meeting held a month before we split the groups, the parents chose the topics. In order to attend, many parents had to leave work early, and they did. The first meeting was huge; 35 moms attended, and 40 dads attended the next day. It was awesome.

The things the men said were truly eye-opening. I found their willingness to be candid very humbling. Following both meetings the parents expressed their excitement, and attendance remained high the rest of the school year. Many personal

53

victories took place, but the one that I enjoyed the most was what a father shared: his wife had learned to let his decisions stand regarding the discipline of their children. She no longer argues with him in front of their children. Praise God!

Well, needless to say, God's Word is true. "And let us not be weary in well doing: for in due season we shall reap [the benefits], if we faint not" (Galatians 6:9, KJV). I'm sure the dynamics may be different in other settings. But it is immeasurably beneficial to get dads involved and to allow God to work through you to improve family relationships and foster a better quality of life for the customers you serve. Among the benefits to our preschool are more content families and parents who enthusiastically participate in the program.

REFLECTION

Creating a Bond Between Parents and Teachers

By Stacia Emerson. Reprinted from *CEE*, Spring 2001.

We've heard the phrase *cutting the apron strings*, often used when sending a child off to school for the first time. What kind of image do you see when you hear that phrase? Taken at face value, the phrase seems to indicate that parents are turning their children over to someone else and letting them make it on their own. This would mean that now it is the teacher's turn to train the child—the parent has nothing more to do with it. But we know that in reality the strings should not be cut but connected to create a strong bond between home and school.

Communicating with parents and encouraging their participation in the classroom should be a priority with all early childhood teachers no matter what age or developmental level they teach. Presented here are some basics ideas for encouraging parental participation. Most are universal and can be adapted according to the need.

Let's Get Acquainted!

It is important to get to know the child and his or her family as soon as possible. For infants, trust between the caregiver and parent must begin to grow. Toddlers and preschoolers also benefit from this early bond. They sense that school is "an OK place" when parent and caregiver interact positively. Getting acquainted can be done in a personal, individual interview at school or in a home visit. It is also helpful to have the parents complete a family background form that includes information about other family members; the parents' work and hobbies; and the child's talents, medical information, and developmental milestones (such as sitting up).

VIPs: Very Important Parents!

Value parents for who they are: their culture, their gifts and talents, their experience, and especially their knowledge of the child. Listen carefully and value their input. It is important to children of all ages to have their parents and caregivers work together as a team.

"Ask and Ye Shall Receive"

Many parents are very willing to participate in school-related events or to volunteer to work with your class if they are aware of the need. Send a checklist, asking parents to indicate areas in which they would like to help. Be specific in your requests and provide clear instructions with the tasks. Don't forget that some parents can help at home by preparing materials for centers—for example, creating newsletters on the computer, or washing the dress-up clothes.

Keep Parents in the Loop

There should be regular communication from school to home and back to school. Create a system for regular contact, and be consistent in using it. A small stenographer's notebook makes a fine home/school journal. Parents write on one side, and the teacher writes anecdotes from school on the other. This practice allows the parent to feel "linked" to the school, and it will give the caregiver helpful insight into what life is like at home. Another way to use the journal is to keep post-it notes handy all day for writing notes to parents, then stick them in the journal at the end of the day. When caregivers take the time to write highlights and milestones such as "Melissa discovered her toes today," or "James helped care for a friend who was hurt," the notebook becomes an important developmental record for the parents.

Take Me Home

Make an effort to send things home that allow the parent to visualize what happened during the day. These could include: cassette tapes with songs and fingerplays children are learning, or with cooing and babbling to record language milestones; photographs of children participating in activities at school or during special events; class books that the children have dictated to the parents; monthly "photo-books" that highlight a unit of study, special event, or field trip; a children's book that you are reading in class; a center activity that can be done at home; and of course all the children's creations. This practice will help the parents feel involved through knowing what goes on during the day, and it will give them plenty to talk about with their child.

"Be Prepared"

Be ready at appropriate times to give parents handouts that deal with developmental issues (such as toilet training) or that may help the family through a difficult phase with their child (the death of a loved one). This practice builds confidence in the parents that the caregiver is informed about relevant is sues, and it continues to build a supportive, trusting relationship.

Show and Tell

Show parents what developmentally appropriate practice looks like, and tell them how you implement it in your classroom. Allow parents plenty of opportunities to observe what is happening in your learning centers, and explain why these activities are important for development. Telling need not be done verbally. Teachers can place signs in learning centers stating the objectives of the center or the particular center activity. Developmental charts and checklists can also be posted in the classroom and given to the parents to take home. When you send home products that are a result of work in centers, indicate how that work fits into the developmental sequence. For example, toddlers taking a page full of scribbles home are in an important stage of writing development. A torn paper collage is an excellent way to promote aesthetic development and practice fine-motor skills. Make sure parents understand the significance of that page of scribbles or those bits of paper by writing a note on the back of their child's page or including developmental information in a newsletter about these specific activities.

Center Visits

Another fun way to *show* parents what developmentally appropriate practice looks like is to allow them to spend time in the center with their child. Highlight a certain center each month, and encourage parents to complete an activity with their child. The experience will be pleasant for both parent and child, and it will certainly allow parents to feel more fully involved as they see first hand what is appropriate at their child's age level.

These basic ideas can help you establish a relationship with parents that connects the apron strings rather than cutting them! "And over all these virtues put on love, which binds them all together in perfect unity" (Colossians 3:14).

58

REFLECTION

Keys to Communication

By Dorothy Brunson, Reprinted from *CEE*, August 2007.

Communication is extremely important for teachers. Good communication is key to building trust between the teacher and the parent. I enjoy watching my early childhood teachers communicate with parents, and I would like to share a few ideas with you.

Preparing for Great Communication

- The teachers start their day by praying for the students and the parents by name. Usually the prayers for parents are general; however, a parent may have a particular prayer need, such as a health issue, a lost job, or separation anxiety, and the teachers pray for those needs specifically.

- Knowing the name of a person communicates that you care about him or her as a person. The students wear name tags at the beginning of the year so that the teachers can learn their names as quickly as possible. Parents are proud of their children and the name they have chosen for them.
- Later, the teachers learn the parents' names as well. Learning the parents' names takes time and a lot of practice, but doing so is very rewarding.

Oral Communication

- The teachers greet the parents and the students daily with smiles, hugs, and warm, welcoming comments such as "I like the beautiful smile you have on today."
- Since we have a half-day program, the same teachers are in the class at pick-up time. The teachers find something positive about each child to share quickly with the parents during pick-up time each day. At times, some children's behavior during the day can make it difficult to relay something positive, but the teachers have found that they can better see the positive when they have prayed for the children.
- The teachers communicate any negative behavior privately and confidentially. If possible, they talk with the parents in a comfortable,

quiet area. The teachers may have to communicate by calling after school hours. In this type of conference, the teachers always start and end with positive comments about the child. Often, the teachers will also start the conference with a prayer. The teachers ask the parents for ideas about how to handle the situation. Sometimes, the parents deal with the same issues at home; sometimes, new problems arise because the children are in a group situation, and the parents have not dealt with that particular behavior issue. Bringing the parents in so that they can partner with the teachers in decision making about the behavior helps the parents feel involved, and they often have helpful insights as well.

- At the beginning of the school year, the teachers and the parents get to know one another during an orientation time. The orientation also allows the teachers to communicate expectations to the parents and give them the opportunity to ask questions about the classroom activities.
- Formal parent-teacher conferences take place twice a year. At these conferences, the teachers communicate about all areas of the children's development.

Written Communication

- The teachers write personal weekly or monthly newsletters to relay information about their classes. The teachers always have another teacher or the director edit the newsletters for spelling and grammatical errors.
- Each class has a parent bulletin board that contains monthly calendars, weekly lesson plans, and newsletters.
- The director sends out a monthly newsletter that relates schoolwide news and events. • The teachers or the director sends out memos to share breaking news when needed.
- For special events, the parents receive postcard invitations.

Our communication to parents is crucial. The parents need to feel connected to the teachers and to their child's class. After all, we are in a partnership, and the parents are the lead. What an awesome opportunity we have to help children become all they can be for God.

Supporting Military Families

By Pamela Flannery, Reprinted from *CEE*, December 2010.

Change can be a challenge for many people, especially military families who move approximately every three years. As educators, we have the privilege of supporting military families by welcoming them and helping them to "normalize" quickly. After we moved from California to Colorado, I worked in a center where I taught prekindergarten. The director would regularly say, "We're so glad you're here." Those five simple words made such a difference in my life as I was adjusting to not only a new job, but a new community.

The Buddy System

One practical way we can help military children normalize is by creating a buddy system. Buddies can introduce new children to classmates, show them around the classroom, and get them involved in activities, especially during outdoor play. We should never assume that friendships will just happen; we need to help each new child connect quickly with friends.

When a soldier is transferred to a new unit, the military provides a sponsor for that soldier so that he or she can acclimate and feel connected quickly. However, the spouse and the children don't have that advantage. A center can make an impact on spouses as well as children by connecting them to others in the center and giving them a warm welcome. It is a great encouragement when directors and teachers take the time to ask how newcomers are doing and what kind of help the center could give.

Whenever a new military family came to our center, I would ask the children in my class open-ended questions to help them understand what our new student might be feeling. As they began to share how it might feel to move to a new city, a new home, and a new school and to make new friends, the children would become excited about meeting their new classmate.

Soldier Appreciation

Selecting appropriate books to read to the class is another way to help a child

assimilate to his or her new school. Wonderful books about the military and soldiers are available to help children understand the price soldiers pay for our freedom. These stories also bring a sense of pride to military children.

Another way to validate children and their parents is by sending a "goodie" package. Whenever a child's parent deploys, I have the children draw a picture for that soldier, and then we write what they want to say to him or her. The children get excited as they place goodies and their cards in the box to mail. And it is priceless to see the excitement on their faces when we receive a letter from overseas and hear how grateful that soldier was for the wonderful surprise package they sent!

Knowing what job a military parent does is also very helpful, because we can discuss his or her responsibilities with the class and let the children know that, because of what that parent does, we are able to enjoy freedom here in America. I give my class examples of freedoms we have in the United States that many other countries don't enjoy. I also explain that freedom comes with a price—a price our military pays every day for us through their sacrifices.

Emotional Healing

It's important for educators to understand that children who have a deployed parent may be dealing with high levels of fear and stress that many other children may not have. After 9/11, I observed children in my class building towers with blocks and then knocking them down with toy airplanes. I sat next to them on the floor as they played, and I asked open-ended questions such as, "How did it make you feel when you saw the towers collapse in New York?" As the children began to share their feelings, I was able to understand their fears and help them through the process of healing. If children in our centers deal with fears like these, how much greater are the fears of military children whose parents may be in harm's way?

One of the many blessings of working in a Christian school is the freedom to pray with our class! Whenever a student's parent is deployed, we display a picture of that soldier next to the American flag. It is a reminder to pray for that soldier each day, and it also helps bring peace to the heart of a child who may be concerned about that parent's safety.

Deployment: Strategies for Working with Kids in Military Families

By Karen Petty, Redleaf Press (St. Paul, MN), 2009, $24.95, paper

Because so many countries are sending soldiers to conflict, Redleaf Press published a much-needed resource to support early educators in serving children of military families. Although not written from a faith perspective, the book's strategies are easily adaptable for a faith-based program. The book has many strong points:

- Much of the material is presented in charts, graphs, and checklists, so it is easy to navigate.
- The appendixes are worth the cost of the book.
- The glossary explains often-confusing military terms and acronyms, so early educators can speak knowledgeably with parents.
- An entire section lists organizations (including websites) that support families during times of separation and further inform the work of early education programs.
- Topics of neglect, separation, and grief are always difficult to approach with parents and families, but this tackles the tough topics with materials and strategies for discussion.
- Lists of children's literature are topically arranged to address each challenging category.
- Because it is a recent publication, it gives up-to-date suggestions on using technology to make separation easier on both children and active-duty parents.

If you have even one child or family from a military background, this book is a worthy investment.

Supporting Families Through Meaningful Ministry

REFLECTION

Make the Connection: Parental Involvement in Education

By Sara Jo Dillard, Reprinted from *CEE*, December 2010.

Moms and dads are excited about their child's early education experience, and so they want to get intimately involved. They long to get to know the teachers and the school administrators on a personal level, as well as the other parents in their child's classroom. Parents also desire to contribute to the school community.

What events and programs can you offer to help parents meet their need to tap into the school culture? As early education principal of Southside Christian School (SCS), I often find myself pondering this question in an effort to help parents get involved. I desire to be intentional in creating opportunities for parents to come together, share their dreams, and discuss their needs while developing a partnership with our school.

Connect Through Events

65

At our school, the early education faculty and staff, the other school administrators, and I have developed various events and programs that give parents opportunities to connect with other families, learn more about parenting, and plug into the school on an intimate level. Early education teachers play a vital role in recognizing and suggesting activities that will engage the parents in a closer relationship with the school while also offering programs to meet their other needs.

Begin by prayerfully seeking God's plan for your school and the needs of your parents. I have experienced God's immeasurable love, and I want our early education parents to feel the school's love for them. As parents raise the future generation, it is my deep desire that each family is fully supported, equipped, and confident to parent from a Christian worldview.

To get started, I suggest surveying your parents to find out their parental needs and their desires for involvement and partnership. Invite a core group of parents to meet with the administration to give input on their expectations and needs.

As you get to know your parents, develop a yearly plan containing opportunities for parents to connect with the school. Keep the venues varied in scope and size to meet the needs of most families.

Promote Connection

Promotion is an important factor to consider when planning events. Promotion should attract the parents and help them see how the event will benefit them personally. Remind parents often about the event in as many formats as possible. Getting a commitment to attend by offering a sign-up sheet or ticket sale can also boost awareness and attendance.

Here is a sampling of events that have been successful at Southside Christian School. Hopefully these will get your creative juices flowing! There are many possible ways to connect with parents. The key is to know what your parents need and how much involvement they desire.

Parenting Seminars

Author and psychologist John Rosemond presented an evening seminar on parenting and family issues, discussed his book *Parenting by The Book* (New York: Howard, 2007), and held a book signing after the lecture. The hour-and-a-half event drew 750 people. This was a schoolwide effort involving a planning committee, ticket sales, promotion and advertising, and complimentary childcare for school families attending the event.

We held a "Parenting with Hope" conference for parents in the community. Dr. Milt Uecker was the keynote speaker for the half-day Saturday seminar. Attendees also selected two additional workshops, and a focused challenge by the school superintendent ended the morning event.

Book Studies

We offered book studies during the summer. Works studied included Rosemond's *Parenting by The Book* and Emerson Eggerichs' *Love and Respect* (Nashville, TN: Thomas Nelson, 2004). Childcare was provided for a nominal fee for the hour-and-a-half morning discussion. About 30 teachers and parents attended the studies during two summers.

Picnics

Early education parents attended a Picnic and Play event where families and teachers met on the playground. Parents brought a picnic dinner, and the school provided games and prizes for the children. This venue created a relaxed atmosphere in which parents could get to know one another and visit with the teachers and school administrators while their children played in a safe environment with friends.

We planned a Homecoming Tailgating Party for early education parents. They munched on foods while watching their children play in a secured area. After eating and visiting with other families, parents and children attended the school's homecoming pageantry and football game.

School Events

We invited early education parents to attend a school concert as a group. Seating was reserved in a special section for attending families. Afterward, many of the families visited a local restaurant for dessert and fellowship.

We arranged group seating for early education families at different school sporting events. Earlier, players from the teams had shared their testimonies during a weekly chapel. Early education children identified with the players during the game because the children had been able to get to know the players during the chapel program.

Chats with the Principal

The early education principal invited parents in at a specific time to ask questions or find out information about the school. Attendance varied according to the date and time of the event.

Field Trips and Classroom Activities

Parents are often invited to fulfill specific responsibilities on field trips and at class events. All parents attending go through a screening process and a background check. Parents get to know the other students and play an integral part in helping the teachers.

Reading Enrichment Program

Parents and grandparents may sign up to read to their child's class. The volunteer program director preselects the books, creates a lesson plan for the reader, and includes a suggested activity in the packet along with the book—giving the readers a readily available, approved reading program.

Volunteers in Partnership

Parents may sign up to volunteer. A school employee—the volunteer and community-relations coordinator—matches parents' gifts and talents with opportunities to help in the school. Parents reap the benefits of helping the teachers, and teachers enjoy having the needed help.

As you plan events for your parents, evaluate the events' outcomes to ascertain whether they are meeting your parents' needs and expectations. Parents enjoy having various options to choose from, and they also want a format that encourages discussion and participation. Make it quick and easy for parents to give feedback on school events and partnering opportunities. Also, school leaders must show genuine concern for parents by listening to and praying with them.

Partnerships develop over a period of time as trust and rapport are built among the parents and school leaders. As you strive to make an impact on the next generation, connecting with parents' needs and interests will play a key role in creating these partnerships. Through these avenues, we create a long-term sense of community in Christian education.

Early education parents who attended some of the above seminars and school events had this to say:

> Tailgating with other early education families during homecoming each year has been a fabulous way to connect with other parents while sharing the excitement of a large, schoolwide event. The strong bonds that are formed between parents in similar stages of life have the potential to be lifelong friendships and major influencers of parenting style. How wonderful that Southside Christian School provides so many opportunities to connect with other Christian families and to share this journey together!

The summer book studies and John Rosemond parenting seminar ... have greatly impacted my life. Not only have I enjoyed getting to spend personal time with early education staff, teachers, and other SCS parents, but the books and subsequent discussions have encouraged me to be a better wife and parent.... I love that the school my children attend encourages me to follow Christ more closely and glorify Him in our home as well as at school. Public schools can't give you that! I think the greatest benefit of attending such events is that we see our children's teachers and the other parents in another setting. We are able to relate to each other as people, personally, not just as "my kid's teacher" or "so-and-so's mom or dad." It really helps create a stronger sense of community at SCS. These events have absolutely helped me focus more on Christian parenting.

Participating in Christian parenting seminars at SCS has been a true blessing to me. What a great opportunity to learn from experts in the field, network with other Christian parents, and gain tools and insights that will last a lifetime!

Participating in classroom activities and field trips with my daughter has been a wonderful experience for me at SCS. Seeing firsthand the quality programs and Christian principles that she is exposed to daily in the classroom reaffirms my strong belief in the impact Christian education makes in the life of a child. As a parent, I always walk away from an event with ideas and tools that I can implement at home to help me on my Christian parenting journey.

I am a big fan of the field trips (as well as all the other volunteer opportunities).... It is such a blessing to share in these educational activities and to see a bit of the teacher-child interaction. It is so awesome to see our children interacting with school friends. I am a firm believer in the partnering of school, church, and family. To be able to see the teachers pray with the children and encourage them while in a learning environment helps us stay connected. Being a part of [our children's] experience enables us to discuss experiences with them later.... Our children spend so much time at school it only makes sense to be involved. We need to support the educators as they support us. We are a team. I think it is a win-win for us to all stay on the same page and pray for phenomenal results. Young people have so many obstacles to overcome these days that the more equipped they are, the better chance they have to succeed.... It is so comforting to know that my children are in a safe, loving Christian environment that they love!

REFLECTION

Love with a Purpose: Helping Preschool Families Deal with Grief

By Danny Oertli, Reprinted from *CEE*, December 2010.

I'll never forget being pulled aside by my daughter Gracie's preschool teacher after class. She took a deep breath, looked me in the eye, and said, "Little Gracie has had a really tough week."

Nothing new; "little Gracie" had always been pretty strong willed. Sensing my embarrassment, she was quick to clarify, "No, not behaviorally, emotionally. She asked me today to make sure none of the other children in class knew she didn't have a mommy."

My heart literally ached for Gracie. Earlier that year, my wife, Cyndi—Gracie's mommy—had passed away of a heart attack at age 30 after a long battle with cancer. Gracie was four at the time and struggling with her new reality. As a newly single parent trying to navigate my way through the preschool years, I would be grateful for the caregivers who showed thoughtfulness—and frustrated with those who didn't seem to understand our unique struggles.

As a caregiver to preschoolers who are grieving, you have the incredible opportunity to be a bright star of inspiration and healing. You can learn from our experience. Here's how.

- **Don't be afraid.** Everyone deals with grief differently. Some like to talk; others don't. But in my experience, most grieving people are frustrated because conversations become so strained, so hands-off. Everyone is afraid to "say the wrong thing." Don't be afraid. Ask how the parent is doing. Ask what the child's favorite memory of his or her deceased loved one is. Yes, there may be tears—but tears are often healing.

- **Find creative ways for children to express their grief.** If children don't want to talk, ask them to share their feelings by drawing pictures or telling stories, or offer to pray with them. Their positive response might surprise you.

- **Understand their fears.** During this period, I found my children's most common fear was isolation. Kids are acutely aware of being different. Find ways to emphasize the similarities they share with classmates. In activities, pair outgoing, friendly kids with those who are hurting. Grieving kids are desperate to find acceptance but often struggle to find it on their own.

- **Understand their exhaustion.** Overwhelming fatigue is common for many single-parent households. Combine that with grief, and you have a very stressed family unit. Knowing why a child may be acting out will help in knowing how to deal with him or her.
- **Create a community of caring.** Our preschool informed the school families of our situation. As a result, many were quick to offer meals or help with childcare, easing the burden.

Years have passed since those difficult days, but the teachers and administrators who showed love and understanding made a permanent impact on our lives.

REFLECTION

Building a Bridge of Trust: The Parent-Teacher Partnership

By Susan Mathis, Reprinted from *CEE*, December 2010.

Three months before I was born, my father died, leaving my mother to raise two children under two—alone. But when I was four months old, my mother, widowed grandma, and bachelor uncle bought a house together. Moreover, they rented out a room to an "old-maid" nurse. Lucky us—my brother and I had not two but four adults telling us what to do! Mom still quips that with all those different—and very diverse—role models, it was amazing we turned out "half normal." But by and large, our early childhood was a happy, well-adjusted one. Somehow we understood the different roles and levels of authority each person held in our lives.

What an amazing responsibility it is to have the opportunity to shape each little life we touch! Like those grown-ups who were so influential in my young life, we teachers and caregivers play an important part in forming children and helping them become who God intends them to be. As we partner with each child's parents, we also help form the child's view of parents and other authority figures and influence the level of respect he or she has for the family.

When I owned and operated my own preschool, one of my primary objectives was to come alongside parents and help them successfully parent their children. I wasn't there for my own agenda but for God's, the child's, and the parents'. My main goal was to serve the families God put in my life, whether I played the role of mentor, teacher, partner, or teammate. Later, when I taught elementary school alongside colleagues who were teaching my children (and I was teaching theirs), I learned to navigate the challenges that arose in partnering with them as a parent and as a colleague. Whether you're a rookie or a seasoned teacher, a parent or a caregiver, discerning how you can best make a difference in each individual life is a recipe for successful ministry.

When a Mentor Is Needed

As preschoolers, my brother and I usually felt quite secure because we knew

73

that, although Grandma and Uncle—and others—gave their opinions on child rearing, they always acknowledged who our parent was. They built a support structure to help my mother raise us well. But whenever the nurse gave her know-it-all opinions on how to raise us, the lines of authority were undermined and our little worlds became confused.

A measure of authority comes with the title of teacher, and I was keenly aware that my education gave me a knowledge of child development, psychology, and early childhood education that parents sometimes didn't have. And sometimes a parent's inexperience caused frustration for me as the child's caregiver.

For example, Jason came to my preschool from a single-parent home. He was far too worldly-wise for his young years, and he was excessively aggressive. At first, I was judgmental about his mother and impatient with him, but soon I remembered that I should "clothe" myself "with compassion, kindness, humility, gentleness and patience" (Colossians 3:12). So I began to befriend Jason's mom, humbly and gently mentoring her in parenting skills, especially when it came to maintaining discipline and imparting social skills.

Although we never spent time together off the school property, we built a mentoring relationship that became an important foundation for the future. Halfway through the school year, I discerned that Jason had deeper issues, and because I had built a place of trust with his mother, I was able to share my concerns. Through a series of events, we discovered that earlier in the year Jason's babysitter had abused him. The compassion, kindness, and concern I showed for that little boy and his mother went a long way in helping them through a terrible situation.

When a Partnership Is Important

I loved to be with my bachelor uncle, who was my Disney-dad father figure. Sometimes he let me do things that Mom might not have, but I always knew who had the final authority, and I knew what "Mom's way" was. And once my uncle knew that my mom didn't approve of something, he supported her decisions. For nearly five years, he partnered with her to raise my brother and me. It was also obvious that Mom respected my uncle for the role he played in our lives and for the sacrifices he made to help her.

Respect and support should go both ways between teachers and parents. Forming a parent-teacher partnership establishes the fact that the child's best interests are at heart. Moreover, it teaches the child how a strong working relationship can be formed. However, that's not always as easy as it sounds. Sometimes parents see their child's teacher or caregiver as a threat to their personal place in the child's life.

Melissa's mom seemed to undermine my authority as a teacher at every turn. When I taught the children how to ties shoes with "bunny ears," she retaught her daughter "the right way" with the "round the tree" method. If I taught sign language to a praise song one way, she had a better way. I felt that she tried to undermine my teaching and that she felt I could do nothing right, so partnering with her seemed impossible. But Colossians 3:13 says to "bear with each other and forgive whatever grievances you may have against one another." So I chose, repeatedly, not to get offended. When Melissa's mom questioned something I taught, instead of getting frustrated and having a poor attitude, I affirmed her as Melissa's mother in front of both parent and child. But nothing seemed to change.

Then Melissa's mom had a marriage crisis, and I had the opportunity to support her through it. Shoe tying and methods of learning no longer became a focal point of contention. During this tough time, Melissa's mother grew to respect, support, and honor me, and I her. In fact, we became friends.

Parents dealing with personal challenges or self-esteem issues can be tough to break through to, but focusing on the common love you have for the child can help build a bridge of partnership. And the child is better for it all—little Melissa blossomed because her mother and I formed a partnership instead of allowing a spirit of competition to poison the child.

When Establishing Teamwork Is Critical

Because my mother worked the 3-to-11 nursing shift, Grandma was my primary caregiver. I was her little shadow and thought of her as my best friend. But I also knew that Grandma was my mother's teammate in raising my brother and me, and I understood that Mom was number one. Although I knew Mom and Grandma didn't always agree with each other's methods (and sometimes they made their differences quite clear), Mom gave Grandma lots of grace—and vice versa—and my brother and I reaped the benefits of that teamwork. Mom and Grandma simply chose to work together to provide an atmosphere of love and care.

Although I didn't realize it then, I now know that forming a team takes recognition of the need, a lot of sacrifice, a measure of unselfishness, and hard work. When I started teaching in the school my children attended, it was a whole new game. As teachers, we were usually united and had lots of grace for one another's idiosyncrasies. However, in one situation with a fellow teacher (and parent), it wasn't easy to deal with issues affecting the children. The other teacher was teaching my son, and I was teaching her daughter. She made it clear that she was a veteran teacher and I was the rookie! Because of these interpersonal complexities and the personalities involved, lines of authority seemed to blur, emotions got in the way, and teamwork became difficult.

Tensions rose to a frenzied level when the other teacher's daughter (who was in my sixth-grade class) cheated on a test, and I caught her. That same week, my son was being silly in reading circle and, when asked why he was misbehaving, said, "Because foolishness is bound up in my heart!" Well, foolishness was in my cheating student's heart too, and I felt an extra measure of mercy might just be the thing to smooth the rough waters both families were facing. After a challenging discussion, my son's teacher and I committed to "let the peace of Christ rule in [our] hearts, since as members of one body [we] were called to peace" (Colossians 3:15). We worked hard to become team players, and the children settled into the school year well.

As we do all we can to humbly mentor our student's parents, as we partner with them, and as we build a winning team for the sake of our children, we will in turn build a foundation of grace and peace on which the child can flourish. In so doing, we parents and teachers can make the school year a successful and memorable one, see our ministry bear fruit, and watch the children blossom into all God intends them to be.

The "New Normal" Family

By Elisa Morgan, Reprinted from *CEE*, December 2010.

Homework paper? Check. Backpack? Check. Jacket? Check. Ooohhh, Friday folder? Check. Overnight bag? Check.

Marcus and I piled into the car with his loot in tow. He buckled himself into place behind me as I backed out of the garage. We sang "Noah's Ark" as we drove the four blocks up the street to his school, where I would drop him off for the day before turning left out of my neighborhood and making my way 15 more minutes to my office. As we pulled into the parking lot, we punched the speed dial on my phone and Marcus' mom answered.

"Hey, buddy! Have a great day! Did you have fun with Yia Yia and BeePees?" (That's "Marcus-ese" for me and his grandfather.) My daughter thanked me for keeping Marcus overnight, and then we hung up and trundled on into his classroom, where he stuffed his supplies in his cubby. Remembering that Marcus would be picked up by his birth father after school, I rehearsed the routine—take your overnight bag, do your weekend homework. With a knowing nod, this little five-year-old assured me he "had it" and turned to join in circle time. I blew him a kiss and headed out.

A normal morning in the life of a normal preschooler. The normal backpack and homework. The normal songs and routines. The normal smooches and hugs. And what has become the normal grandparent-mom-stepdad-birthparent-community family of the preschool-age child. I never saw it coming, but here it is— and I'm living it out full-time.

The New Normal

Maximizing the impact of teaching on a child in early education today means normalizing that young child's "new normal" family. Less than 62 percent of children live in what is defined as a traditional family—a household headed up by the child's two married, biological (or adoptive) parents. About 23 percent live full-time with their single biological mom and 3 percent with their single biological dad. Fifteen percent of all children live in blended families with a stepparent, stepsibling, or half-sibling (Kreider and Fields 2005).

Sure, there are still tons of intact, two-parent, married families in our world. Their enduring legacy is valued and foundational for the family. But the family today is characterized by increasing diversity in structure and blend, and the successful early education teacher will learn to work within this "new normal." How might teaching be shifted to meet the needs of adopted or special-needs children or those from single-parent or blended families? What symptoms and signals might be watched for? What testing or evaluation might be applied? What tactics support children in new normal families to have the best learning experiences possible?

To get our bearings, let's look at some normalities of today's new normal family.

Single-Parent and Shared-Parenting Families

Forty percent of first children are born outside marriage when the mother is under 30 (Bachu 1998). One out of 4 children lives in a single-parent home, and 1 out of 25 lives with neither parent (Kreider and Fields 2005). Many in this last category live with a grandparent, while some are in foster care.

The response for the early education teacher?

- Two sets of communication folders
- Two conferences for many children, or four schedules to align for one conference
- Two sets of Mother's Day/Father's Day/Christmas gifts—and the resulting challenges of where to shelve them all and which to hand out to whom for taking home
- A place to corral overnight bags
- Emergency forms with extra lines and spaces for all the necessary phone numbers and e-mail addresses

- Detailed documentation of the various legal rights of each parent—and special care given to those who may be allowed only carefully supervised parenting time
- Charts of who should be called when the child runs a temperature—on which day of the week and which week of the month—and who is allowed (or not allowed) to pick up the child

While the child may obliviously continue on his or her way, the teacher must take great care to dot the i's and cross the t's to accommodate the hidden needs in the shared-parenting family.

However, many single parents are also solo parents. In such cases, the mom, dad, or custodian must perform the work of both parents—full-time. Exhaustion, stress, emotional needs, loneliness, and financial struggle abound. How is one parent to cover multiple school activities, conferences, volunteer efforts, and fund-raising activities while holding down one and sometimes two jobs to pay the bills? Early education teachers succeed in meeting students' needs by being intentionally sensitive to such matters and learning to accommodate the ever-adjusting realities of these parents.

Cohabiting Families

Nearly one in 20 children (5 percent) now lives in an unmarried-couple household (Casper, Cohen, and Simmons 1999). In such homes, the institution of marriage is variably respected. Some couples are not married because of philosophical reasons, some because they lack the commitment necessary for marriage, and some for purely economic reasons. While most Christian schools probably have fewer cohabiting parents, trends show that in the buster generation, even followers of Christ register less concern about this pattern (Barna 2006). The prepared early education teacher will realize that she or he is serving a young population whose values may allow for such a new normality. Children may possess hyphenated last names or last names different from their mother's or even their father's.

Grandparent Families

In the United States, 8.6 percent of all children live with at least one grandparent, and almost a quarter of these have no parent in the home (Kreider and Fields 2005). Life with a preschooler is challenging enough when you are a relatively young parent. Grandparents who are parenting face additional challenges that require extra sensitivity from teachers:

- An unexpected and new season of child-rearing responsibility

- Increased physical challenges and depleted energy
- Challenging interactions with parents who are out of the responsibility loop
- In some cases, a lack of legal authority for decision making
- Financial challenges

Such concerns are sometimes offset by seasoned parenting skills, patience, and networking—but teachers are wise to turn up their sensitivity dials in cases where the new normal life of their students includes living full-time with grandparents.

Adoptive Families

Through public, private, stepparent, international, and grandparenting relationships, 1.4 million American children—almost 2 percent—live with at least one adoptive parent (Kreider and Fields 2005). While some cases of international or cross-racial adoption are easy to spot, many other adoptive situations may be impossible to detect.

What difference does it make? It's important to understand some of the unique realities inherent in adoption. Both parents and children are affected by and process through seven core lifelong issues: loss, rejection, guilt and shame, grief, identity, intimacy, and mastery and control (Silverstein and Kaplan 1982). While adoptive children often succeed well in education and in life, certain "unseen" possibilities should be evaluated, such as the incidence of learning disabilities, genetic issues like hearing and vision impairment, and health-related challenges. Emotional issues such as attachment disorders may also play a part in a child's life at school. Privacy policies may make it impossible to discover the specifics of a child's home life, but the sensitive teacher will keep possible scenarios in mind when customizing instruction and interaction with each child.

Redeeming Families

Whatever our experience with—or value judgments on—today's family, new normal families are no surprise to God. God made the family. We might typically think of pre-Fall Adam and Eve strolling through the Garden of Eden as the prototypical family that all other families should resemble. But both Old and New Testament biblical families are as ripe with diversity as the new normal family is in our world today. In Scripture, we find families built with love and chastity, but also families formed from rape and sin, children born from one father to mothers who were sisters, children born out of adultery, and children born to people of humble means and then relinquished for others to raise.

Throughout all generations, God's love and provision for children continues, despite specific family dynamics. While children surely benefit from the intact union of parents who lead them forward under biblical guidelines, every family can be a redemptive launching pad for life.

Children need safe communities of learning in order to grow and develop. Whether educating others' children or raising our own, we can maximize our investment by recognizing and respecting the unique elements of today's new normal family. When we bring an attitude of love, sensitivity, compassion, flexibility, and watchfulness, and we are ready to customize instruction to the unique needs of today's family, we create a community where all children can thrive.

Percentage of Children Ages 0–17 Living in Various Family Arrangements: 2001

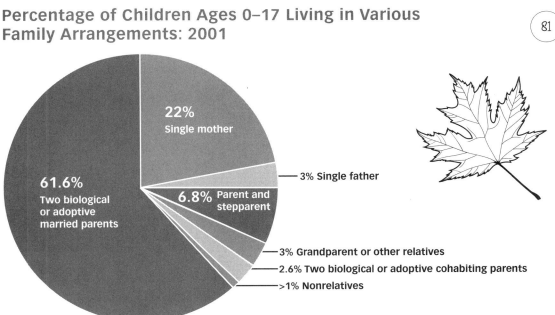

Source: Adapted from U.S. Census Bureau, Survey of Income and Program Participation, 2001 Panel, Wave 2

References

Bachu, Amara. 1998. Trends in marital status of U.S. women at first birth: 1930 to 1994. Population Division Working Paper No. 20, U.S. Census Bureau. Paper presented at the annual meeting of the Population Association of America. http://www.census.gov/population/www/documentation/twps0020/twps0020.html.

Barna Research Group. 2006. A new generation of adults bends moral and sexual rules to their liking. http://www.barna.org/culture-articles/144-a-new-generation-of-adults-bends-moral-and-sexual- rules-to-their-liking.

Casper, Lynne M.; Philip N. Cohen; and Tavia Simmons. 1999. How does POSSLQ measure up?: *Historical estimates of cohabitation*. Population Division Working Paper No. 36, U.S. Census Bureau. Paper presented at the annual meeting of the Population Association of America. http://www.census.gov/population/www/documentation/twps0036/twps0036.html.

Kreider, Rose M. and Jason Fields. 2005. *Living arrangements of children*: 2001; Current Population Reports, P70-104. Washington DC: U.S. Census Bureau. http://www.census.gov/prod/2005pubs/p70-104.pdf.

Silverstein, Deborah N. and Sharon Kaplan. 1982. Lifelong issues in adoption. Adoption Media. http://library.adoption.com/articles/lifelong-issues-in-adoption.html.

REFLECTION

Section 2 Authors

Darlene Buchanan Bladon, AA, has served at Frederick K. C. Price III Preschool in Los Angeles for the past 30 years, 21 as director. Before that, she taught with Los Angeles Head Start for 9 years. She is a nationwide seminar speaker for Willie George Ministries.

Dorothy Brunson, BS, serves as the early childhood director at Rocky Mountain Christian Academy Preschool in Longmont, Colorado. She has been involved in preschool education for more than 20 years, and she has written curriculum for early childhood education.

Paula Cowart, MEd, has served in multiple roles within early education. Before moving from Kansas City, Missouri, to Memphis, Tennessee, Paula served as director of Little Learners Preschool. She now enjoys teaching third grade at Evangelical Christian School in Eads, Tennessee.

Sara Jo Dillard, MEd, is beginning her 20th year of service at Southside Christian School in Greenville, South Carolina. She has a passion to connect with and minister to her early education parents. She also serves on the ACSI National Accreditation Commission and teaches workshops and seminars at ACSI conferences and conventions.

Stacia Emerson, PhD, has served in multiple roles within early education: a teacher, a Sunday school teacher, and a college professor. She is currently a professor at Texas Wesleyan University.

Pamela Flannery, BA, has been a children's pastor for 9 years and a master teacher for 6. She has earned a degree in biblical studies and her director certification. She received her mentor teacher certification in 2000 in Northern California. Her current home is in Colorado Springs, Colorado.

Jim Ed Hardaway's passion as a speaker, a writer, and a dreamer is fueled by 20 years of ministry to students and adults searching for authentic adventure in God. He is founder, creative designer, and lead writer of Epictrek.com, and he has spoken at Evangelical Press Association and ACSI conventions for his creative innovation and his experience in reaching twentysomethings. He gets a thrill out of playing his Fender Telecaster, hiking, and mountain biking. He works at Compassion International and lives in Falcon, Colorado, with his wife, Tonya, and their three sons.

Teena Ingram has served in her current position as director of the Highlands Christian Preschool in Calistoga, California, for more than 20 years. She has contributed to ACSI's ministry as a conference presenter, an accreditation evaluator, and an area leader. Additional Virtue Tree resources can be found at www.KidShapers.com.

Leanne Leak, BA, serves as ACSI's Western States Early Education Field Director. Leanne is conversant in early education policy, accreditation, and she maintains her knowledge base in early education through continual reading, synthesis, and study. She is in the process of completing a graduate degree.

Becky Lockwood, BS, thrives on teaching four-year-olds at Southwest Christian Academy in Fort Worth, Texas.

D'Arcy Maher, MEd, serves as ACSI's director of Early Education Services. She is also the managing editor of *Christian Early Education* magazine.

Susan Mathis, BA, taught school for 13 years. She was the founding editor of *Thriving Family*, and she also edited 11 other Focus on the Family publications. Now, through SM WordWorks (mathis.wordworks@gmail.com), she writes, edits, coaches writers, and serves as a consultant to Christian publications. She is enjoying her granddaughter, who was recently born in South Africa.

Elisa Morgan, MDiv, is publisher of *FullFill* (www.fullfill.org) and author of *She Did What She Could* (www.sdwsc.com). She is also president emerita of MOPS International, wife of Evan, mother of Eva and Ethan, and Yia Yia to Marcus.

Danny Oertli is an accomplished singer, a songwriter, and an author. Danny loves chocolate shakes but has never eaten ketchup, ever. He lives in Parker, Colorado, with his wife, Rayna; their three children; and Ranger the beagle. For booking information and product orders, please visit www.dannyoertli.com.

Section 3:
Parent Education Resources

Patient Parent vs. Pushy Parent

By Milton Uecker. Reprinted from *CEE*, Special Parents Issue 2002.

Parents are God's instruments for raising and nurturing children. As such, parents are constantly making decisions, some having consequences that are of minor importance and others setting courses affecting the character and personality of the child.

The choice of an educational philosophy and program for the early childhood years (birth through age seven) is critical, because the child's initial academic experiences are directly linked to self-concept, attitude toward school and learning, and a successful foundation for future academic endeavors. The basis of this decision, like many others, should rest on a thorough knowledge of child development and of the nature and needs of each child. Psalm 139 draws attention to God's intimate knowledge of each individual. It is this knowledge of unfolding development and individual makeup that enables God to father us so perfectly. This knowledge begins at conception and extends through all the stages of our lives. God's choices for us are based on His perfect love and desire to grow us to fullness. However, parents must guard against choices that are motivated by parental goals, which are sometimes selfish, rather than by goals directed solely toward creating a healthy childhood. Life in Christ includes focusing on the needs of others, and the members of our own family are the first and primary "others" in our lives.

Schools often fall into a similar temptation. In their joint statement on "Reading and Pre-First Grade," the American Association of Elementary/Kindergarten/ Nursery Educators, the Association for Childhood Education, the International Reading Association, and four other educational organizations stated their concerns related to preschool curriculum trends:

Decisions related to schooling, including the teaching of reading, are increasingly being made on economic and political bases instead of on our knowledge of young children and how they best learn. In a time of diminishing financial resources, schools often try to make "a good showing" on measures of achievement that may or may not be appropriate for the children involved. Such measures all too

often dictate the content and goals of the programs. In attempting to respond to pressures for high scores on widely used measures of achievement, teachers of young children sometimes feel compelled to use materials, methods, and activities designed for older children. In so doing, they may impede the development of intellectual functions such as curiosity, critical thinking, and creative expression, and at the same time promote negative attitudes toward reading. (Association for Childhood Education International 1979)

This statement—written more than 20 years ago—instead of being outdated is amplified in today's quest for academic excellence. Today's parents have increased the pressure on schools to provide early academic acceleration. This pressure, even though well-intentioned on the part of parents, is increasingly the deciding factor in designing the learning environment and outcomes for early childhood. At the very time when educators are being encouraged to develop programs according to a research knowledge base, early educators continue to ignore what has been shown to be the best practice in early childhood education, and instead they substitute it with activities and curriculum designed for older learners. Even Japan, a country that we often try to emulate academically, spends only one percent of preschool classroom time on academic endeavors. The Japanese Ministry of Education has six primary goals for preschoolers. Three of the six include fostering habits and attitudes needed for a healthy, safe, and happy life; fostering an interest and concern about language and a cultivation of enjoyment in talking and listening to language; and fostering a richness of emotion through diverse experiences (Lewis 1995). Play and other group interaction are thus the dominant activities.

A young child is at a distinct stage of cognitive and brain development. Preschool children "speak as a child, think as a child, reason as a child" (1 Corinthians 13:11, NASB). They are not miniature adults, so their classrooms and academic interactions must be designed for the immature learner—not the mature learner.

Young children use perception as their basic tool for taking in information. As children interact with their environment through their senses, they collect information and form concepts. These concepts are later represented symbolically through oral language and finally through the written word. New concepts are communicated symbolically, through language or print, only when children have experienced the ideas concretely and have a concept for each word used. Therefore, before children can learn through oral or written input alone, they must have a rich background of concrete experiences during which information was taken in perceptually by manipulating objects and observing relationships in the environment. Meaningful learning relates to what is already known through prior experience. Oral language is the means of expressing and testing new ideas and concepts. As children hear new ideas and interact orally about them, often during play, they are learning to think and use information. Therefore, skill with oral language precedes skills in reading and writing and should be the focus of early education curriculum.

Accelerated preschool programming, often referred to as academic preschool, operates under the assumption that four- and five-year-olds have both a full storehouse of concrete experiences and the oral language fluency to learn through a symbolic, literate, and passive means. Children are viewed as having perceptual skills that are developed enough to begin reading and writing. In reality, because of television and computer "screen time," the language base and thus the readiness base of children today is less than in previous decades (Healy 1999). It is not unusual to find five-year-old children struggling to speak in complete sentences. Nevertheless, children who are not yet speaking fluently are placed in learning environments where the outcomes focus on formal reading and writing. Rather than evaluating children's readiness and placing them in programs accordingly, educators assume readiness, and children become frustrated in the resulting learning process.

89

A program that is more child sensitive, or focused on a developmental understanding, views children as moving through stages of intellectual, physiological, and social development. Because of individual timetables, children vary greatly in their perceptual ability—that is, auditory and visual perception and memory, visual-motor ability, fine- and gross-motor coordination, and language development. Students are grouped according to their readiness for learning various skills. They are actively involved in manipulating concrete objects, observing, experimenting, explaining ideas, and predicting outcomes. These programs operate under the assumption that when ready, children will work with greater ease and acquire greater understanding. Stress is placed on listening, gross-motor activity,

oral language development, and a minimal amount of pencil and paper work. In a child-sensitive approach, children who demonstrate readiness for early literacy are given opportunities to learn to read, while those without the readiness base are given time and opportunities for growth.

A Christian philosophy of education "aims to help the student develop his personality based on a proper understanding and acceptance of himself as a unique individual created in the image of God and on the fullest possible development of his own capabilities" (Garrick 1978). Both the parent and the school must therefore view the child as an individual. Parents must know their child, evaluate readiness, and select a program that will nurture and grow their child—not rush her toward failure. Geraldine Steensma, in her classic on Christian education, expresses this objective well:

> Each student is a unique creation. He will have more ability to perform in one skill
> than another; he will reach different levels of performance than other students;
> he will need to proceed through his learning his way. Individualizing instruction
> in skills recognizes that each student is a unique creation. (Steensma 1971)

Application of this truth requires a program different from one in which all children are expected to do the same thing in the same way on the same day. David Elkind has labeled this latter type of education as "miseducation." Miseducation during the early stages of psychosocial development can lead to a child's perception of self as incompetent, and it places his or her initiative, industry, and sense of belonging at risk (Elkind 1987). Within the early childhood classroom, developmental variance and individual giftedness require diversity of both activities and expected outcomes.

Parents must choose an appropriate classroom for their child's early education. Learning must be nurtured rather than forced. Teachers can move children forward along a developmental timeline, but they cannot re-create the timeline:

> To think of the student as an object for forming is to deny his being and his office.
> As a creation of God, called to a religious office, no human being can be an object.
> A human being is always a subject. Any other part of creation may become an
> object for man's forming, but not his fellowmen. This principle defines the limit of
> responsibility for the educator in her task. (Steensma 1971)

Children are a gift from God. They are His design, and each child differs in personality, developmental timetable, and gifts. Parents have high hopes and aspirations for their children, and with God's help and leading, these hopes will be realized. But sooner isn't always better than later, and stress is a poor substitute for the joy children can experience during their initial years of learning. What will you choose to do—develop or accelerate?

References

Association for Childhood Education International. 1979. Reading and pre-first grade. *Childhood Education* 02:289.

Elkind, David. 1987. *Miseducation: preschoolers at risk*. New York: Knopf.

Garrick, Gene. 1978. Developing educational objectives for the Christian school. In *The philosophy of Christian school education*, edited by Paul A. Kienel. Colorado Springs, CO: Association of Christian Schools International.

Healy, Jane M. 1999. *Failure to connect: How computers affect our children's minds and what we can do about it*. New York: Simon and Schuster.

Lewis, Catherine C. 1995. *Educating hearts and minds: Reflections on Japanese preschool and elementary education*. Cambridge, England: Cambridge University Press.

Steensma, Geraldine J. 1971. *To those who teach: Keys to decision making*. Terre Haute, Indiana: Signal.

REFLECTION

REFLECTION

How to "Stress Proof" Your Child

By Mary Campbell. Reprinted from *CEE*, Special Parents Issue 2002.

Many young children today are exhibiting symptoms of excessive stress. As Christian parents and caregivers, we need to be aware of stress' symptoms in young children, understand what causes it during the early years, and know how to protect children from its devastating effects.

People of all ages experience stress, but it is often overlooked in children. Children who are experiencing stress often demonstrate changes in behavior, including regression. Some symptoms of stress are more serious than others, and no child will exhibit all of them. Nevertheless, the following partial list of symptoms in children is helpful: stomachaches, headaches, nervous blinking or twitching, inability to sleep, nightmares, sleeping too much, anger, restlessness, aggression, disobedience, uncooperativeness, depression, accident proneness, frequent urination, frequent crying, fearfulness, mood swings, whining, nausea, nail biting, thumb sucking, bed wetting, frequent infections, disruptiveness, pulling hair out, refusal to eat, eating too much, clinging to parents, lying, stealing, loss of interest in a favorite activity, and cruelty to animals.

Once the symptoms of stress are recognized and potential causes of stress are identified, an effective approach to this serious issue includes several steps: consider what can be done to prevent stress from occurring in the first place, identify methods that will support children during both chronic and acute stress, and develop strategies to help children during traumatic events, which are often intensely stressful. It is God's desire and plan for His children of all ages to live and walk in peace. He wants us to bring the little children to Him so that He can bless and protect them with His perfect peace and gentleness (Mark 10:13–16).

Stress is a mental or physical tension or strain. Some stress is unavoidable and may be healthy when limited. The baby playing peekaboo tingles with excitement and wonders, *Will she be there next time or not?* This activity is actually important for promoting brain growth and development, since synapses, or brain connections, are made and strengthened through this and similar activities. The preschooler anticipating an exciting field trip or a birthday party shivers with delight as he looks forward to the event, his excitement building. These are examples of good stress and are not harmful when experienced in small doses.

Problems occur when children feel overwhelming and unchecked stress from neglect or during chronic or acute situations. The greatest protection from harmful stress and the effects of traumatic events for babies is a strong emotional bond with caregivers. This bond results from warm, responsive care and is essential for healthy emotional and brain development. Infants need many smiles and hugs and much time and attention. They need to have their needs attended to promptly—to be fed, changed, and cuddled regularly. Caregivers also need to talk to and provide stimulating sight and sound to children to protect them from stress.

God created our bodies with an adrenal system that causes the release of hormones intended to give us extra strength during stressful situations or danger. The adrenal glands produce cortisol, often called the stress hormone, in both adults and children. In adults, stress and the hormones it releases appear to increase the incidence of heart attacks, strokes, and many other physical manifestations and problems. Studies have shown that neglected or abused babies have a much higher cortisol level because of the acute stress and that continued exposure to this hormone leaves their brains measurably smaller. Babies who experience too much stress and trauma are more likely to demonstrate hyperactivity, anxiety, poor emotional control, and other mental and emotional illnesses later in life.

Young children can suffer from chronic stress, acute stress, or both. Some causes of chronic stress include neglect, exposure to violence in the home or community, drug or alcohol abuse in the home, too much academic pressure, too little free time, overscheduling by caregivers, parental work pressure, harsh or authoritarian punishment practices, long illnesses, excessive restrictions and reprimands, academics that are not developmentally appropriate, fear of failure, financial pressure in the home, poor nutrition, poverty, loneliness, and ongoing verbal or physical abuse. Children can become overwhelmed with stress because of life situations, particularly sensitive temperaments, or even behavior patterns of well-intentioned parents and caregivers. Then these children may suffer from fear, guilt, and emotional or physical damage. Frequently, acute stress reactions occur in young children who face major events and life changes, such as a death in the family, separation or divorce, remarriage, an automobile or other serious accident, a serious illness or surgery, a geographical move, a change in caregiver, sexual or physical abuse, the incarceration of a parent, the birth of a sibling, or the loss of a beloved pet.

Just as we gain a perception of what we look like by seeing our reflection in a mirror, children perceive our treatment of them as a reflection of what their worth is and what they are like. According to psychologist Eric Erikson, emotionally healthy preschoolers will want to create, explore, play, and try new things. When adults place excessive restrictions on children or criticize their actions, these children believe they are inadequate and they develop a sense of guilt, which will lead them to believe they are bad people. They also suffer from impaired emotional growth. Children whose activities are harshly criticized or regularly discouraged will suffer from the effects of stress, developing a poor self-concept that will be long lasting. In contrast, encouragement and gentle sensitivity toward young children can build a hedge of protection around them.

Often children are overlooked during times of crisis—times when they need help the most and when they may be carrying enormous burdens of grief and anxiety. During traumatic life events such as death, divorce, moving, remarriage, a long illness, or the change of a significant caregiver, children suffering from acute stress find it much easier to cope when a parent or significant adult takes time to talk to them, sensitively explaining the circumstances. Consistent support and ongoing caring communication greatly reduce anxiety and grief in young children.

Loving parents and caregivers should be alert for symptoms of stress in their children, carefully monitoring their own behavior to be certain that they provide a calm and nurturing environment. The most important preventative steps we can take to "stress proof" little children are introducing them to Jesus, teaching them that He loves them just as they are, and helping them understand that He is with them in every circumstance. Then we need to pray for the children daily and ask God to help us see each one—through His eyes of love and compassion—as a priceless treasure that is wonderfully and fearfully made. As we see each child as a special and unique creation with a divinely appointed purpose, God will begin to flow through us in new ways that minister peace to children.

How to "Stress Proof" Infants and Toddlers

DO	DON'T
Cuddle, touch, and hold infants	Be afraid to spoil an infant by holding her
Pick up quickly and comfort when crying	Let infants "cry it out"
Provide visual, tactile, and auditory stimulation	Keep children in cribs or playpens in drab surroundings with littler interaction
Respond to infants in affectionate, nurturing ways	Fail to respond to smiles, fail to talk to babies, or fail to carry them
Provide immediate attention to needs for nourishment, elimination, cleanliness, and warmth	Neglect babies and fail to provide prompt attention for nourishment, elimination, cleanliness, and warmth
Assure loving relationships with primary caregivers	Have frequent changes in caregivers
Encourage exploration and autonomy	Restrict exploration and autonomy
Provide quiet times and independent play	Allow unlimited noise or restrict time for independent play

How to "Stress Proof" Preschoolers

DO	DON'T
Model kind and respectful behavior and treat children with loving sensitivity	Show impatience, be impolite to children, or embarrass them in front of others
Practice smiles, gentle humor, and laughter	Frequently frown and give looks of disapproval
Speak with a kind and gentle voice	Raise your voice or yell across the room at a child
Discipline by rewarding good behavior	Use severe punishment to control behavior
Use encouragement and praise to show love and acceptance of children	Focus on what children are doing wrong and reprimand regularly
Reward effort	Demand perfection
Tell children they are special to you and to God	Tell children that they are bad or that they never listen
Plan developmentally appropriate activities	Push children academically
Plan plenty of opportunities for play with other children	Severely limit children's time for play with other children
Avoid public comparison of children using charts, checks, stickers, etc.	Compare children's academic success or behavior publicly on charts, boards, etc.
Explain in advance when stressful events are pending, and provide reassurance	Withhold explanation about pending stressful events such as moves or changes
Provide opportunities for creativity, exploration, and new activities	Restrict or harshly criticize creativity, exploration, and attempts at new activities

References

Black, Janet K., and Margaret B. Puckett. 2001. *The young child: Development from prebirth through age eight*. 3rd ed. Upper Saddle River, NJ: Prentice-Hall.

Dobson, James. 2002. Solid answers. *Focus on the Family* (June).

Elkind, David. 1988. *The hurried child: Growing up too fast too soon*. New York: Addison-Wesley Publishing Co.

McCracken, J. B. 1986. *Reducing stress in young children's lives*. Washington DC: National Association for the Education of Young Children.

Trawick-Smith, Jeffrey. 2000. *Early childhood development: A multicultural perspective*. 2nd ed. Columbus, OH: Merrill (Prentice-Hall).

97

REFLECTION

REFLECTION

Raising a Musical Child

By Catherine Santander. Reprinted from *CEE*, Special Parents Issue 2002.

There was nothing different about Michael's infant and toddler life. He fell asleep to lullabies and passed his days with *Sesame Street* songs. At 18 months, though, he experienced his second Christmas, and we experienced the beginning of a new, musical life.

One of the gifts he received that morning was a small, colorful xylophone, and he spent most of the day playing with it. As the weeks passed, whenever we created a story, we used the xylophone for sound effects. We slid the small plastic mallet up the scale to illustrate a character climbing a hill, and we pounded the lower notes to represent a giant entering a room.

That year we watched Michael equate music with everyday actions. One day as he sat on the floor marching his toy firefighter up and down the steps of his toy firehouse, he adjusted the pitch of his voice to mirror the action his toys took on the steps. He raised his voice higher as he bounced the firefighter up the steps and lowered his voice as he brought it back down.

It was fun to watch his development, and we, of course, joined in. We lowered our voices as we walked downstairs. We knocked on doors with rhythm! We clapped, tapped, and slapped on everything! We bounced balls loudly, softly, quickly, and slowly; and we bounced them in steady rhythms of *bounce, catch, bounce, catch*, matching words with patterns.

On his second birthday, my sister gave Michael a music stand, a book of J. S. Bach's piano suites, and a conductor's baton. Family members joked, "Is he supposed to play that?" No, he wasn't supposed to play that. However, Michael knew what he could do with it. He could *imagine*. We assembled the music stand in his bedroom, and he did the rest. He spent hours strategically placing his stuffed animals in front of himself, conducting them from behind his music stand by waving his baton.

Soon Michael wanted to create musical instruments for his new orchestra. We filled Tupperware containers with beans, rice, and dried noodles for shakers, and we used wooden spoons to investigate the different sounds of our pots and pans. Every empty paper towel or toilet paper roll became a flute, a clarinet, or even a kazoo.

What God had placed inside that little boy was flowing out, not because of what we had done, but because of who Michael was. We were not making a musician; we were observing a child and participating in what God had already placed in him.

When Michael was two years old, I walked outside one day to call him for lunch. As I approached him, I watched him methodically breaking off almost every tiny twig that protruded from a stick. When he had the stick looking the way he wanted, he placed his mouth over a small twig near the top and hummed while his fingers danced up and down the 12-inch stick. Then he caught a glimpse of me, and with a sparkle in his eyes that I will never forget, he turned, looked up, and said, "Look, Mom, I made a bassoon!" I sat on the grass with him that afternoon, and he enthusiastically played his new instrument for me.

At the end of age three, Michael began cello lessons. The cello was so tiny— one-tenth the regular size—and Michael squeaked out a few songs with great pride and joy. Was he the star student or a child prodigy? No. Did he love it? Yes.

As Michael grew, everything became music. Our home vibrated with the tapping of his musical patterns on every part of our furniture, on every part of his body, and from every configuration his mouth could make.

He stopped lessons for a few years in elementary school and again at the beginning of high school, but the music always called him back. Now in college as a music education student, he plays every instrument in the orchestra and performs in a string trio, an opera orchestra, and a symphony orchestra. His main instrument remains the cello, and he continues not as a lover of performing, but as a lover of music. He told me once, "I want to be the first person to place an instrument in the hands of young children and inspire them to become passionate about music."

Every time I hear Michael play, I thank God for him. And when that six-foot-one, dark-haired boy of mine rises in his black tuxedo to take his final bow, I rise to my feet, eyes filled with tears, and still hear him say, "Mom, I made a bassoon!"

Appropriately Engaged or Playing Helicopter?

By Ken Smitherman. Reprinted from *CEE*, November 2007.

In the early education program, parent involvement is valued and necessary. We want your active involvement. But I want to challenge your thinking just a bit, so my question is, Are you establishing negative habits that might become barriers when your child enters formal education? I was intrigued to discover online a number of humorous, not so humorous, and serious categories of parenting. Among this list, I discovered hyperparenting, lifelong parenting, parallel parenting, financial parenting, stealth parenting, and helicopter parenting. Perhaps the last, helicopter parenting, is simultaneously the most and the least humorous.

According to Wikipedia, the web-based interactive encyclopedia, the following definition articulates this unique parenting style:

101

> A helicopter parent is a term for a person who pays extremely close attention to his or her child or children, particularly at educational institutions. They rush to prevent any harm or failure from befalling them or letting them learn from their own mistakes, sometimes even contrary to the children's wishes. They are so named because, like a helicopter, they hover closely overhead, rarely out of reach whether their children need them or not. An extension of the term— "Black Hawks"—has been coined for those who cross the line from a mere excess of zeal to unethical behavior such as writing their children's college admission essays. (The reference is to the combat helicopter of the same name.)

What then might you as an *appropriately engaged parent* consider? Pursue a *partnership* with your program. The program is not in existence to take over the parenting role, but to provide support and expertise that will complement your parenting role. It is never intended that the Christian early education program should function in isolation or apart from the family.

At the Association of Christian Schools International, we have identified four crucial areas of learning across all ages served by Christian schools:

- academic/thinking
- worldview
- spiritual formation
- skill development

Let's consider the broad goals of the academic/thinking area. Christian school graduates should be well prepared in all academic disciplines; be skilled in reading, writing, speaking, listening, and thinking; and be proficient in mathematics and science. They should appreciate literature and the arts and understand how these express and shape an individual's beliefs and values; have a knowledge and an understanding of people, events, and movements in history (including church history) and the cultures of other peoples and places; value intellectual inquiry and have the ability to engage in the marketplace of ideas; and appreciate the natural environment and live as responsible stewards of God's creation.

What do these goals look like in early education? What are the appropriate expectations, and does the program you've chosen articulate those expectations well? How can you partner with the program to support your child's readiness for formal education? What can you do at home to enrich this foundational experience?

Give thoughtful consideration to how you can help your child in these academic/thinking areas. Does your home environment encourage inquiry and investigation? Is the question, Why? answered honestly—or is it brushed aside as inconvenient (or irritating)? Do you extend learning by capturing teachable moments? Do your family excursions include children's museums, the library, and other venues specifically designed to engage your child? Rather than hovering at the door of your child's classroom, how can you focus on creating a platform for learning at home? Do you discuss your concerns about your child's development with her teacher?

Partner with your Christian school. It is not a heliport. It is a place where jointly you and your school can effectively "train a child in the way he should go" (Proverbs 22:6).

Effectively Communicating with Your Child's Teacher

By Carol Kautz. Reprinted from *CEE*, March 2006.

Parents are God's principal vehicle for the teaching and the nurturing of children. The Bible tells us in Proverbs 22:6 and 29:17, "Train a child in the way he should go, and when he is old he will not turn from it" and "Discipline your son, and he will give you peace; he will bring delight to your soul." The apostle Paul reminds parents in Ephesians 6:4 and Colossians 3:21 that they are to train and teach their children in such a way that the children do not become exasperated, embittered, or discouraged. In many places in both the Old and the New Testaments, we are told the purpose of this training and nurturing: that we and our children will trust in God, revere Him, obey His commands, and so become holy as He is holy (see Deuteronomy 4:9–10, Psalm 78:4–7, 2 Timothy 3:16–17, and Hebrews 12:5–10).

A critical role of an early education center is to support and strengthen the family unit, to work alongside the parents in teaching and nurturing their children. However, in order for a center to do that most effectively, regular and open communication must exist between parents and teachers. I recently asked our staff to share one or two tips they would like to remind parents of to keep the lines of communication open. Here's what they said:

- Tell me the names or nicknames and the relationships of significant people in your child's life so that I can better respond when your child refers to them.

- Tell me the key phrases your young child uses to express important needs, such as going to the restroom or getting a drink of water.

- Don't assume I always know what's going on between your child and a classmate, and don't wait until a concern or a situation is almost overwhelming before you ask me about it.

- If you have a question about the class schedule, a certain activity, my discipline style, or my behavior expectations for students, please ask me— not another parent.

103

- Please read carefully all written communications posted or sent home by me or the office. We understand that you can feel overloaded, but a lot of important things go on at school, and we want you to know about them!

King Solomon reminds us in Ecclesiastes 4:9–12 that two are better than one and that three are even better. Parents and teachers working together, with the help of the Holy Spirit, will most effectively ensure that our children grow "in wisdom and stature, and in favor with God and men," as Jesus did (Luke 2:52).

REFLECTION

The Pitfalls of Overscheduling Our Children

By Carol Kautz. Reprinted from *CEE*, March 2006.

I read or heard recently that many of us gain our sense of worth through the amount of activity we are involved in. If our workday is not filled with appointments and tasks, or if we find ourselves with time on our hands, we don't feel important or useful. If our evenings aren't filled with meetings, if we're not chauffeuring our children to sporting events or some kind of lessons or a friend's house, or if our weekends aren't overscheduled with family events, we feel as if we've failed somehow. I have to admit that I am one of those people. I find it hard to relax and enjoy a quiet moment. In fact, my niece laughs at me when I tell her I don't get movies to watch at home because there are no commercials breaks, which I use for reading magazines. And I have to remind myself frequently that my worth doesn't come from the things I do. It comes from who I am. More specifically, I have worth because the Lord says I do—because I am His child through Christ Jesus.

Our society is filled with messages and pressures that seem to tell parents that their worth comes from the accomplishments of their children. Children, we are told, must have particular kinds of sensory stimulation throughout their early years (even prenatal months) in order to do well in school. They must read before kindergarten. We feel obligated to enroll our children in organized sports, music, dance, or even karate lessons. If we're not careful, we become their social secretaries rather than their parents. This overscheduling is not God's way. The psalmist describes the raging world around us in Psalm 46 and declares that God is our refuge and strength in the midst of that rage. In verse 10 of that Psalm, God admonishes us, "Be still, and know that I am God." Paul reminds us in Ephesians 2:10 that "we are God's workmanship, created in Christ Jesus to do good works, which God prepared in advance for us to do." This verse applies to children too. And we won't know God's plan for us or for our children if we don't know how to take time to be still before Him and learn to hear His voice.

There is a particular pattern to the development of children. In the early years, children must achieve a strong sense of trust, autonomy, and initiative to most fully develop as healthy older children and adults and to be able to hope in God, turn their wills over to Him, and actively seek out and pursue His purposes for their lives. This optimum development comes from having reliable, consistent adults in their lives and from spending more time in initiating play and interaction on their terms than in pursuing structured, adult-led activities. Children need unstructured time to discover and interact with the world around them, practice their emerging skills on their own schedule, and gain many enriching yet low-key experiences that enhance vocabulary and concept acquisition.

What was that phrase of long ago? "Stop and smell the roses" is how I think it went. God says, "Be still, and know that I am God." He wants a relationship with us and our children—a relationship that is hard to develop in the fast-paced, "doing is better" society we live in. But give it a try. In due time, and through that relationship, our kids will grow to become God's workmanship, not our workmanship, and we will all reap the benefits.

REFLECTION

Meeting Your Child's Need for Love

By Carla Foote. Reprinted from *CEE*, May 2008.

Editor's Note: Starting with an introduction by Carla Foote, this article contains an excerpt from the book *What Every Child Needs: Meet Your Child's Nine Basic Needs for Love* by Elisa Morgan and Carol Kuykendall.

Children have needs, and as parents you want to meet the needs of your child. But often in the daily schedules of life, it is easier to focus on meeting your child's physical needs through meals, nap times, and laundry than it is to focus on meeting the more important need for love. *How do you meet your child's need for love?*

Certainly, hugs are a part of your child's need for love, but beyond the hugs, there are nine ways that you can provide a great foundation of love in the life of your child: belonging, security, affirmation, discipline, guidance, respect, play, independence, and hope.

The following information on children's need for belonging comes from the book *What Every Child Needs* by Elisa Morgan and Carol Kuykendall (1997).

A child's need for belonging is met in the family structure. To build a family with room for all, consider certain blueprints in the construction.

Home as a Haven

"There's no place like home!" Dorothy whispered as she journeyed back from Oz to her home in Kansas. Ahhh. We all know the truth and comfort of that statement. It means walking in the front door and smelling a savory soup that's been simmering on the stove, or the scent of freshly baked cookies that tells us someone has prepared for our arrival! It means sitting in a circle on the floor in front of the fireplace, playing games and laughing together. It means Saturday morning snuggles in bed or celebrating family birthdays with balloons at breakfast.

A good home underlines and emphasizes the belonging of all who enter. Like a welcome mat that pronounces a greeting, this home ushers all members safely inside where they can be refueled and refreshed for living in the everyday world. Children cling to the idea of home as a haven and place of nurture. (69–70)

Families of All Designs

Not all families look alike. Some include married parents, and others single parents. Some boast an only child while others have multiple siblings. Some are built by blood and others through adoption. Still others extend their boundaries to include several generations.... Whatever the makeup of your family, recognize it for what it is: a family!... Families are a God-designed structure, intended to be a haven and meet the need for Fit-Me-Into-the-Family Love. (71)

Tools for Building Belonging

Here are a few tools to communicate a sense of belonging to your children:

Parental Legacy

You have a personal history to offer your child; including him in yours will help him build his own. Pull your little ones up on your lap and open up the storybook of your own life. (72)

Grandparents

Grandparents offer many gifts to a family. If your children's grandparents live far away, consider "adopting" grandparents in your neighborhood. Their influence is important, so receive them eagerly and with joy! (73)

Sibling Loyalties and Sacrifices

Siblings and parents make sacrifices for each other. A mother bringing a new baby home helps a toddler make this adjustment by spending extra special time with the older child to meet his needs. The toddler begins to understand that his mother needs to meet different children's needs at different times, which means not every child is treated equally all the time. It's part of the reality of belonging in a family where everyone learns to sacrifice for each other. (75)

Getting to the Heart of Fit-Me-Into-the-Family Love

Children hunger for a sense of belonging. They display it as soon as they impact the family with their arrival, their newborn needs demanding that family members make some adjustments and make room for them. As [parents], we often feel like construction site managers, in charge of this responsibility of making sure the baby feels welcomed into the family structure. We juggle responsibilities, family schedules, and baby feedings, so that the home will be a haven for all. As children grow up, we use the tools of family traditions and celebrations, reunions and special meals, chore charts and photograph albums. We build this sense of belonging in order to meet their need for Fit-Me-Into-the- Family Love. (80–81)

Reference
Morgan, Elisa, and Carol Kuykendall. 1997. *What every child needs: Meet your child's nine basic needs for love*. Grand Rapids, MI: Zondervan. Mommy,

REFLECTION

REFLECTION

"Mommy, What Are You Eating?"

By Carla Foote. Reprinted from *CEE*, November 2008.

I distinctly remember the first time I realized that my preschooler had invaded my snacking space and that I would not be able to enjoy a candy bar any longer by myself. We were driving down the highway, my preschooler safely strapped into his car seat. I quietly unwrapped a miniature Snickers bar, ready to quickly pop it into my mouth, when my son said, "Mommy, what you eating?"

Yikes—lying to my child wasn't a good option, but I was at least a smart-enough mother to know that if I mentioned candy, the next thing out of his mouth would be a loud, "Me want candy!" And our quiet drive down the highway would deteriorate quickly.

Of course, I can justify my eating habits by saying I don't have a candy bar every day, but the truth is that I do struggle with healthy eating and activity and the struggle affects my body image. And preschoolers observe and copy everything they see us do, say, and eat. So our habits become their habits—the healthy habits and the not-so-healthy ones. Because of the intense scrutiny by our young children, we as parents worry about transferring our own issues about our body image to our children. Whatever your issues with your body, the preschool years are a great time for family activities that reinforce healthy body image for everyone in your family.

Get Moving

Children know how to jump and move and wiggle and dance. As adults, sometimes we have to give ourselves permission to participate in active play with our children. The more your family can enjoy a variety of physical activities together, the better the family members will feel about their bodies—parents included!

Activity doesn't have to be complicated. Try a simple family routine of walking around the block after dinner to get fresh air and exercise, or moving to music in the living room. Put on the bike helmets and have tricycle races to the end of the block. Movement is life for preschoolers, so encourage their movement and participate along with them. A side benefit to active movement is less time for television viewing,

which is a passive activity that exposes children to advertising images containing subtle but often unhealthy messages about body image.

Use Good Fuel

Active children who are using their bodies become thirsty and hungry. Positive messages about using our bodies also spill over into topics about fueling our bodies. Thirsty preschoolers naturally gravitate toward juice products, but the American Academy of Pediatrics (AAP) cautions that fruit juice and fruit drinks are easily overconsumed by young children because those beverages taste good (AAP Committee on Nutrition 2001).* A better choice for active families is a piece of fruit for a snack and water to quench the thirst.

Give Positive Messages

Keep conversation about body parts positive. Preschoolers are naturally inquisitive and observant. If they see you being comfortable in your own body, they will think that being positive is a normal way to relate to their bodies. If they hear you talking about your body in a way that is negative, they will internalize the negative message.

The Bible also has great, positive body-related messages that we can share with children in an age-appropriate way. As you read the creation story in Genesis, you can talk about the amazing way that God created our bodies. Let your preschooler notice interesting things about his body, such as the way his fingers wiggle, or the way he can hold a crayon and draw, or the way his voice can whisper or shout. Affirming to your child that he is "wonderfully made" helps build a great foundation for your preschooler (Psalm 139:14).

Grow Together

Developing a healthy body image is a lifelong process for you and your children. When you focus on the process, rather than a single conversation, you will feel relief from some of the pressure to get it right at every moment. At the same time, you can be purposeful about continuing to grow as a family in terms of positive body image. As your children grow and develop additional physical abilities, adapt your family's

activity schedule to include fun, noncompetitive games and outings that build on your children's strengths and interests.

*The American Academy of Pediatrics reaffirmed its policy on fruit juice in October 2006. To see evidence of the reaffirmation, visit http://aappolicy.aappublications.org/cgi/content/full/ pediatrics;119/2/405.

Reference

AAP Committee on Nutrition. 2001. The use and misuse of fruit juice in pediatrics. *Pediatrics* 107, no. 5 (May): 1210–13. http://aappolicy. aappublications.org/cgi/content/full/pediatrics;107/5/1210.

Additional Reading

The Wide-Eyed Wonder Years by Lorilee Craker (Grand Rapids, MI: Revell, 2006) offers practical and humorous insight into navigating life with preschoolers. Her chapter entitled "Beyond Cereal, Grilled Cheese, and PB&J" offers perspective on finicky eaters. The book is available in retail bookstores or through the MOPShop at www.MOPShop.org. [Editor's note: It was rereleased as *Loving Life with Your Preschooler* in 2008.]

REFLECTION

REFLECTION

Roots of Green Values

By Carla Foote. Reprinted from *CEE*, March 2009.

As you parent young children, how do you go beyond the lists of ways to go green and build a family foundation that is honoring to God's creation? Living green is in vogue now—for children, families, communities, and churches. We recycle newspapers, take cloth bags to the grocery store, and look for ways to minimize waste. But what core values can we model to our children so that even as the technology of recycling and energy conservation changes, they can understand the underpinnings of responsible stewardship of our resources?

First of all, the core value we have as Christians of caring for the earth is based not on a love for this planet above all but on our love for God, who created and "saw that it was good" (Genesis 1). God also gave us stewardship over His creation. We model this care for the earth in how we act and in how we talk about the natural world. Young children have an innate love for nature, and they desire to play with the simple toys of creation—sticks, rocks, bugs, dirt, and water. Rather than restricting these impulses, make space in your home life for plenty of this kind of play. Pair these natural activities with conversations about the amazing things that God created in the world so that your children can begin to understand that their delight in the natural world is based on an appreciation for God's creation.

Another way to value resources is to make choices to live simply. Whether this lifestyle means having a less-crowded schedule, choosing family time at home over costly entertainment excursions, or making conscious decisions about consumer purchases, a simple lifestyle is less resource intense. Over time, choices that simplify our lives result in fewer trips to the store, fewer purchases, and less consumer packaging to recycle. The core value that a simple lifestyle communicates to our children is that people are more important than things. Having neighbors over for a soup dinner and board games is less resource intense than driving to a movie and buying dinner. Along with building community in your neighborhood, such choices communicate the value of relationships over entertainment.

Fewer errands by car can help the environment, your budget, and your health if you choose walking or biking instead. A walk to your neighborhood library is definitely green. Borrowing books is less consumptive than purchasing books, and walking is healthful and nonpolluting. If you live in an area that offers public transportation, take your children on the bus for outings or errands. You'll find that when you ride the bus, you have time to talk with your children and perhaps even read a book during the ride or make up stories since you don't have to pay attention to the traffic. Yes, such trips can be time-consuming, but if you've consciously simplified your schedule, then you may find the time to invest in these activities.

Involve your children in discussions about your family's choices, at the level that is developmentally appropriate for your children. Making your children part of the process not only educates them but also helps them understand the big picture. Then, rather than nagging your children about closing the door to keep the cold air out of the house, your children will begin to understand how small actions such as quickly closing doors can help save energy.

As your family begins to acquire positive environmental habits, watch for creative ways that your children can be a part of brainstorming more ways to save energy or water resources. While you might not want to implement their suggestion of "no baths" in order to save water, perhaps agreeing to bathe in an inch less of water is a step that can accomplish observable conservation.

Consistent habits and activities that are easy to integrate into your life go far in creating the foundation for a lifestyle that honors God's creation. If recycling and environmental concerns are only occasional special projects for your family, then the values reflected by these projects will not become a core part of your children's lives. One-time events can be educational and informative, but it is the daily and weekly habits of stewardship of resources that will build values over time.

REFLECTION

Cornering the Market: Out-of-the-Box Possibilities

By Carla Foote. Reprinted from *CEE*, May 2009.

Our front-porch chairs came in a great big box that was full of play possibilities. After unpacking the furniture, we considered the best home for the box. Rather than breaking it up for the recycle bin, we decided to find a family who would enjoy playing with the box. Sitting on the front porch, our teenagers reminisced about various boxes that had been playhouses, stores, and restaurants. Meanwhile, my husband went across the street to a family who has a three-year-old and offered the box treasure. The answer from the parents stunned us: "No thanks, we really don't want a box to play with." We felt sad for their child, but my husband—not to be discouraged—continued down the block to some parents who happily embraced the play possibilities and took the box to their basement.

Imaginative play is about possibilities—about being transported to a faraway time or place, or even somewhere beyond time and place! Children possess an amazing capacity for imagination and creativity. As parents, we should have a primary goal of fostering an environment in which our children can allow their creative potential to flow. Even though children definitely have the potential for imaginative exploration, the adults in their lives can maximize that creativity by giving them permission to do imaginative activities, places in which to do them, and parent participation.

Permission and Places

Although a chaotic environment is not conducive to family life, some space for messy activities and ongoing projects offers an invitation to creativity. You'll have to determine your family boundaries and tolerance for creative messes. If at least one corner of a room can be project central, then children have a place where they can focus their activity and can exercise some control over their space.

Also consider the focal point of the space where your family most often gathers. If television, electronic games, or computers are the focal point, then those sources of entertainment may distract young children from a rich imaginary world and may draw them into a passive spectator role. Use the off button, and intentionally put electronics in closets or otherwise out of view to minimize the competition for your children's attention.

Along with permission and a physical space, children need spaces in their schedules to daydream and create. Be conscious of the pace of family activities, and know when to decline playdates or other obligations in order to provide some precious hours for imaginative play.

Participation

Getting down on the floor and playing with your children is an excellent investment in family time. As you enter the world of play, remember to follow your children's cues and to participate rather than direct. Children enter into play with no agenda and with a sense of the now, not the future. When they are creating imaginary scenarios, there are no limits, so guard against squelching the fun with too much reality, other than by establishing necessary safety rules.

In addition to spending time with parents in imaginative play, it is also good for children to have time and space to create by themselves, or with siblings or other playmates, while you monitor their activities without being directly involved. If your children continually want your involvement in their activities, set a timer, and tell them that you will join them in a specified time, such as 10 minutes, after they make up a story to act out. Then when the timer goes off, keep your word. Set aside your work, get on the floor, and focus totally on the story they have developed with their puppets, stuffed animals, cars, blocks, or other toys.

Playthings

Keep your imagination corner well stocked with the raw material for creative child's play—cardboard, boxes of various sizes, colored paper or fabric, paper bags, and simple, age-appropriate raw materials such as modeling clay, art supplies, and blocks. Supplement by providing natural objects such as sticks, rocks, and leaves. Look in the recycle bin to find items that can become imaginary props.

Along with finding the mostly free or low-cost raw materials for creative play,

look for open-ended toys that are an investment in a variety of play situations. For example, building blocks offer more possibilities than small play sets, and puppets invite more interaction than stuffed animals.

As you participate with your children in imaginative play, you may find that the creativity provides benefits in your own life and work. Or you may just rediscover the joy of the Creator, since our creativity is just a small mirror of God's creative nature.

REFLECTION

REFLECTION

Program or Process: Spiritual Development in Our Children

By Carla Foote. Reprinted from *CEE*, December 2009.

In the complexities and responsibilities of parenting, it is appealing to think that if we could figure out the right *program* for parenting, all our problems would be solved. However, I think it is more realistic to think of parenting as a *process* rather than a *program*. Especially when it comes to the spiritual development of our children!

Although this statement may seem overly simplistic, just spending time talking with our children can be a key to spiritual development for them. As we talk about the small and large issues of each day, we have an opportunity to help our children understand life in the context of our faith in God. When we talk about a sick friend, we have an opportunity to reassure our children of God's care for this person. When we talk about the thunder and lightning, we can talk about the amazing creative power of God.

In the Bible, the Israelites were reminded of this matter-of-fact way of growing in faith. They were told, "Talk about [God's commandments] wherever you are, sitting at home or walking in the street" (Deuteronomy 6:7, The Message).

This daily interaction in our children's lives multiplies over time—that's the process part of spiritual development. We have 365 days a year with our children. Any "program" for spiritual development would probably take place for only one hour 52 times a year. Just think of the power of your daily program for spiritual development in your children—you have more than 1,800 days with your children from birth through age five, and more than 6,500 days with them in 18 years!

What to Do Daily

A great place to start is at the family dinner table. Mealtime provides a time each day, or at least most days, when the family gathers, takes a few moments to thank God, eats, and talks about the ups and downs of the day.

When your children are preschoolers, family meals may not seem like relaxing, value-infused times; but the consistency, the safety, and the focus of this time are

powerful day after day after day. It is worth the effort of getting children to sit and eat, talk and listen for a few minutes. There is a growing body of research showing the value of family mealtimes in preventing many negative behaviors in children and teens (AboutKidsHealth 2008; CASA 2007).

Along with having a meal together daily, some families may read a Bible verse or pray for children in some other part of the world. Other families may choose to emphasize a conversational approach to the events of the day, helping children put these events in the context of God's involvement in the family members' everyday lives. Even if the conversation doesn't seem overtly spiritual, the time for relationship, connection, and encouragement become part of the process of children's absorbing faith and values from their parents.

Actually, Jesus used this "daily meal approach" to spiritual development with His followers. Many of the biblical teachings of Jesus take place while He ate food with friends or with the multitudes, and we even find one recorded incidence of cooking food for the disciples (John 21:9–10). Jesus understood the simple but powerful impact of shared time together in building faith.

122

Mom, what does your child need most?	Mom, what helps meet your child's needs?
Me!	Counting to 10 a lot
My eyes, my ears, my arms, my heart	Listening
Hugs	Watching
Patience	Being honest about my needs
Acceptance	Accepting myself
To feel important	Using a softer tone of voice
A sense of belonging	Being a child with my child
A sense of humor	Going with my instincts
A mom who knows she has needs too	Tearing up my to-do list
Home–a safe haven	Being able to forgive—again and again
Strings and wings	Turning off the TV
Common sense	Taking a nap so that I'm rested
Prayer	Using an answering machine more often
Laughter	Using a microwave
Routine	Using paper plates sometimes
Firm boundaries	Noticing when my child does something right
Flexible edges	Letting God love me
To know that Mom and Dad love each other	Asking a more experienced mom lots of questions
Answers (Why is the sky blue? Where do freckles come from?)	Seizing the moment
Freedom to fail	Never giving up
Love, love, love	

—chart adapted from Morgan and Kuykendall 1997, 5–6

References

AboutKidsHealth. 2008. What's for dinner? Self-esteem, literacy, and curtailed high-risk behaviour. AboutKidsHealth. July 10. http://www.aboutkidshealth.ca.

CASA. See National Center on Addiction and Substance Abuse.

Morgan, Elisa, and Carol Kuykendall. 1997. *What every child needs: Meet your child's nine basic needs for love*. Grand Rapids, MI: Zondervan.

National Center on Addiction and Substance Abuse. 2007. T*he importance of family dinners IV*. New York: National Center on Addiction and Substance Abuse at Columbia University.

123

REFLECTION

124

REFLECTION

Parenting Through Pain

By Carla Foote. Reprinted from *CEE*, March 2010.

Unexpected events that intrude into our lives can quickly upset the rhythm and daily routines for preschoolers and their families. Getting the phone call that an elderly parent is dying, receiving notice that a job is ending, or hearing an unfavorable diagnosis can lead to significant stress for both parents and children. After the initial shock, figuring out how to navigate both the personal and the family ramifications of a crisis situation can be overwhelming.

Each person will have a different emotional, physical, and practical response to crisis, but I'd like to share a few principles that helped our family navigate such situations when they invaded our lives.

Communication

As parents, often our first impulse is to protect our children from difficult information. Certainly we need to keep our discussions age-appropriate and not overburden young children with adult levels of stress. However, children are very astute about the home's emotional climate, and if they receive no communication about problems, their fears may escalate. A simple, direct conversation at a time when you can sit with the child and be close is the best way to communicate difficult information.

Even if your child has no immediate reaction to what has been communicated, it is helpful as a parent to remain open to questions from your child. These questions might come days or even weeks later and may seem unusual to you because they spring from your child's perception of the event. For example, after a young friend of ours was tragically killed, several months later my daughter asked specifically about what had happened to his body. She was trying to sort it out in her mind, and she needed more information. I really didn't want to relive the tragedy, but I answered her question as honestly and simply as I could.

Along with clear and honest communication within your family, involve your child's teachers and give them the information they need to support your child appropriately.

Reach out

During a difficult family time, it is tempting to retreat behind closed doors and not let friends and neighbors even know about our pain. However, the healthiest way for your family to navigate difficult situations is to reach out and be open to receiving help. Most friends are willing to help, but they may not know your specific needs. Ask someone to take your children for a couple of hours for a play date on the weekend so you can have a physical and emotional break. By recognizing your own needs and asking for support, you will be better equipped to persevere.

Routine

Young children (and adults) derive emotional health from the predictable routines of their day. Mealtime, nap time, reading time, cuddle time, and bedtime are markers in their lives that provide consistency and a sense of security. As much as you realistically can, continue these routines even when confronted with personal or family crises. Familiar patterns will contribute to your family's emotional health..

Additional Reading

Carol Kuykendall's book *Five Simple Ways to Grow a Great Family*, available at MOPShop.org, will give you tools to strengthen your family for times of both joy and pain.

Some crisis situations require professional resources. Ask your school for referrals to local mental health professionals to get the resources you and your family may need to thrive. MOPS.org/help also has resource articles for many difficult situations, such as grief and economic hardship.

REFLECTION

"But Mom, You Promised!" The Responsibility Gene

By Carla Foote. Reprinted from *CEE*, May 2010.

My daughter was in charge of scheduling students for volunteer service in high school. Often she would bemoan the fact that people would sign up for service hours and then cancel because they had something come up or a "better opportunity" for their time and attention. For some, sleeping in on a Saturday might trump a volunteer activity! She noted that she had never been allowed to cancel out of commitments, because our family had what she called "the responsibility gene." She asked me how this trait of keeping commitments had become a hallmark of our family. As I reflected, I realized that the responsibility gene originated long before my daughter's high school years.

The root of building responsible young adults lies in the early years of family and parenting, when we are in daily interaction with young children. Simple standards of keeping your word and telling the truth—for both children and parents—set the foundation for taking responsibility in age-appropriate ways throughout our lives.

Keeping Commitments

For a young child, an example of this type of interaction might be keeping a commitment such as going on a play date or to a birthday party. After a child has committed to another person, backing out of the event is not a responsible option, even if the child receives an invitation to something more fun—like a trip to the zoo. Lack of responsibility also devalues our relationships with other people, because we don't care enough to keep our word to them. A young child may not be able to fully understand how another person's feelings are hurt by this lack of commitment, but a parent can use this as a teachable moment.

Ask your children questions to help them process this idea for a particular situation: If you do not do _____ (commitment) how will _____(affected person) feel? How does it feel to you when _____ (turn the situation around to them)?

Parents also model this for children, who are watching us carefully and noticing when our stated values don't line up with our actions. Telling the children's ministry coordinator that I am sick with a cold and can't help in the nursery, when really I just would rather not get up on Sunday morning, will undermine any statements I make to my children about the value of responsibility.

Being Honest with Children

Developing lasting values such as responsibility can feel daunting for us as parents, because we know that we are imperfect people and we won't always be consistent in our own actions. Acknowledging our own shortcomings in front of our children promotes honesty and openness. When we realize that we have not lived up to our word or values in an area such as responsibility, we can be honest with our children and admit that we made a bad choice. Such honesty goes a long way toward modeling both the character trait we are working on building and the honesty that our children need. It also demonstrates the importance of choices and of asking for forgiveness when we have wronged someone.

Instilling Respect and Responsibility

Often, parents of young children emphasize the direct-skill areas—such as tying shoes, putting toys away, and learning letters and numbers. All of these skills are important for young children, but deeper values such as responsibility and respect for others in relationships are lifelong skills that will enable our children to grow and adapt in a changing world. The specific skills your four-year-old will need when she is 24 are hard to anticipate. Our world is changing so rapidly that our children will need skills we haven't even imagined. I didn't know 20 years ago how many different technologies there would be to communicate with people. However, I do know that respect and responsibility are qualities that will demonstrate character and build positive relationships with people, regardless of how much the world changes. Instilling character traits such as responsibility will transcend time, culture, and a changing world.

Section 3 Authors

Mary Campbell, PhD, has served as a teacher, an administrator, a college professor, and a college dean at the undergraduate and graduate levels. As a gifted writer and teacher, she has developed curriculum and traveled internationally to train teachers in ministering effectively to young children. An artist at heart, she now spends her retirement in her studio interpreting the ordinary into beautiful works of art.

Carla Foote, MA, is director of communications for MOPS International. Carla enjoys providing resources to equip women for all the seasons of their lives. Even though her children are in college, Carla still loves reading children's literature—especially to children.

Carol Kautz, MEd, is the founding director of Calvary Children's Center, a weekday ministry of Calvary Church in Naperville, Illinois. Besides enjoying her opportunities to watch young children and help them grow, Carol enjoys presenting at workshops and seminars to help teachers and parents grow.

Catherine Santander taught preschool and kindergarten for 13 years while raising three children who all enjoy the performing arts.

Ken Smitherman, LLD, was President of ACSI for 13 years. Prior to coming to ACSI, he provided educational leadership as a teacher, a principal, and a school superintendent. He also served as vice president of CRISTA Ministries (an organization that includes nine separate ministries) in Seattle, Washington. Now retired, he enjoys time with his wife and high school sweetheart, Karen, and with his children and grandchildren.

Milton Uecker, EdD, is academic dean for the graduate school at Columbia International University in Columbia, South Carolina. He has served in educational programs for more than 40 years as teacher and administrator in schools in Korea, Texas, and Virginia. He earned his doctorate with an emphasis in early childhood education.